The End of
Work-Life Balance

Stefan Osthaus

Copyright © 2014 Stefan Osthaus

All rights reserved.

Photo credit: istockphoto.com

ISBN: 1495366987

ISBN-13: 978-1495366987

ACKNOWLEDGMENTS

I would like to thank you—the readers of this book—for the invaluable feedback you have been providing while on your quest for better Life Balance. Balanced people make for a better world!

My thanks also goes out to the thousands of employees I have been fortunate enough to work with during my career. You created the environment in which much of the advice from this book had been developed and tested.

Last but not least I would like to thank my wife, my family, and my friends for the profound conversations that led to this book becoming a reality.

CONTENTS

Part 1 *Introduction* _____ *1*

   1. Why Work-Life Balance Is Dead _____ 2
   2. How to Improve Your Life Balance _____ 7
   3. How to Use This Book _____ 11

Part 2 *Life Balance Advice for Yourself* _____ *15*

   1. Find the Time _____ 16
   2. Do You Get Enough Tranquility? _____ 19
   3. Important Things First _____ 23
   4. Block Time for Important Things _____ 26
   5. Shut Up Your Gadgets _____ 29
   6. Introduction to Meditation _____ 32
   7. Working from Home Is Not Easy _____ 43
   8. 1,000 Places to See Before You Die _____ 45
   9. Workout Music in Style _____ 47
  10. Stop Wasting Time at Your PC _____ 48
  11. Remote Troubleshoots _____ 50
  12. Values, Ethics, Faith, Religion _____ 52
  13. Too Much Suffering in the World? _____ 55
  14. Are You Two Kinds of Happy? _____ 58
  15. Look Up for Motivation _____ 62
  16. Treat People with Kindness _____ 65

17.	Depolarize	67
18.	The Book of Awakening	69
19.	The Diamond Cutter	71
20.	A Very Pragmatic Approach	73
21.	Preview Your Deathbed	76
22.	Beyond Religion	79
23.	Guide to the Bodhisattva's Way of Life	81
24.	De-Clutter Your Lifestyle	83
25.	When in Debt, Change Your Life	87
26.	Review Your Recurring Spending	90
27.	Self-employed and Successful	93
28.	Are You Relatively Poor?	95
29.	Don't Fly Blind Financially	97
30.	Do You Have the Right Home?	100
31.	My Home is My (Affordable) Castle	101
32.	De-Clutter Your Life	105
33.	Is Your Home a Chore or Hobby?	107
34.	Commuting to Work	109
35.	Get a Robot to Help in Your Garden	111
36.	A Space Age Vacuum Cleaner	113
37.	When Being Healthy Is Not Achievable	115
38.	Sleep Well	117
39.	Thoughts Before You Sleep	119
40.	Eat Well and Exercise	121
41.	Explore Alternative Medicine	123
42.	Stop Sitting	124

43. Don't Worry About Stress _____125
44. Your Recharge Toolbox _____128
45. Burn Away Your Mosquito Bites _____131
46. Is Your Scale Online? _____133

Part 3   *Life Balance Advice for Your Relationships* __135

1. Alone Time With Your Partner _____136
2. Trip of Love—Looking for Places to Go? _____138
3. Time Without Your Devices_____143
4. Plan Your Vacation Carefully _____145
5. On People Who Want to Be Unhappy_____148
6. Caring For Your Elderly Parents_____151
7. Hands-Free Timesavers _____154
8. The Five Essential Truths About Friendship ____155
9. How to Make New Friends _____158
10. The Five Essential Things to Maintain Friendships _162
11. Tools for Staying in Touch _____166

Part 4   *Life Balance Advice for Your Work* _____169

1. Reduce Your Worklist _____170
2. Decide When and Where You Work! _____173
3. 15 Things to Work Smarter _____175
4. Delegate_____178
5. Make Sure You Like Your Work _____180
6. Dealing with Email: Manage the Flood _____182
7. Dealing with Email: Tune Your Spam Engine____186

8. Dealing with Email: CCs Go Separate _____188
9. Dealing with Email: Stop Using (Most) Folders_____190
10. Dealing with Email: Know Your Device _____195
11. Dealing with Email: Working with Your Admin ____197
12. Dealing with Email: Being a Good Email Citizen ___200
13. Easily Create Meaningful Agendas _____206
14. Managing Meetings Across Time Zones _____208
15. Only Have Efficient Meetings _____211
16. Have a Three Minute Version _____213
17. Make Your Breaks Social _____215
18. Share Your Screen During a Phone Call_____217
19. Working in a Global Team _____219

Part 6   Resources_____225

1. Your Life Balance Improvement Plan _____226
2. Your Coupon for mybalance.net _____232
3. Recharge Toolbox Tear-Out Sheet _____233
4. About the Author_____235

Part 1 Introduction

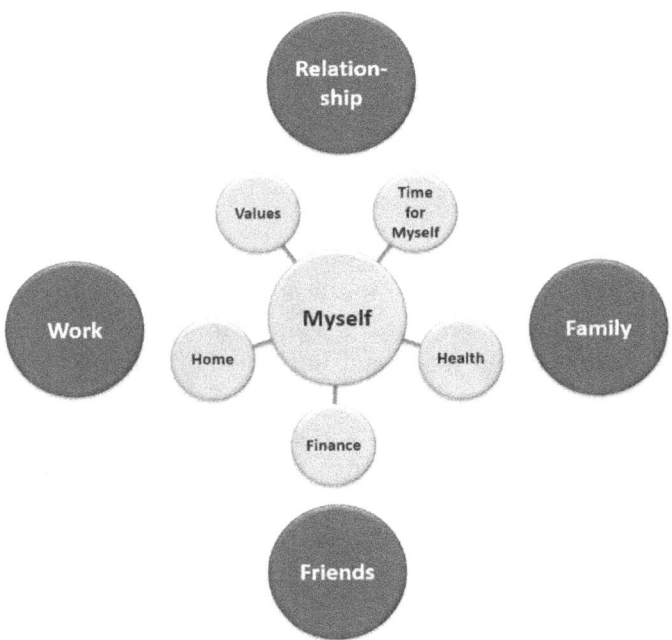

1. Why Work-Life Balance Is Dead

On the Topic of Life Balance

The first step toward improving bad work-life balance is dropping the term!

In my research, one complaint employees consistently made was the lack of a good "work-life balance." This complaint is right up there with bad pay, inadequate budget and the occasional complaint about the manager.

Why is it that we view work as standing opposite of life? What can help us improve the balance in our lives? And can we learn to drop the term "work-life balance"?

Work Is Bad – Life Is Good?

If we view Mondays through Fridays, eight to five, as the bad times in our life and only the weekends and evenings as good, this means we're spending a major part of our lives suffering, not advancing our goals and not pursuing what we find truly satisfying and meaningful. To balance this lack of fulfillment, we may find ourselves trying to compensate on the weekends with over-consumption, distractions and entertainment. Or we do the opposite: vegetate on the sofa to recover from our work week. It's little wonder if this model leaves us unsatisfied—fortunately, life is much more versatile than that!

The Good Things in Life Come in Five Buckets – Introducing Life Balance!

If we look at our lives holistically, we can see that work is an important part of our well-being. So are people such as our partner, our family and our friends—they all play a huge role in how we feel about life and ourselves. Last but not least it is us who determine to a great extent what life means to us and the quality of life we lead. Balancing these five areas—us, relationship, family, friends, and work—will allow us to attain Life Balance and live a purposeful and fulfilling life. Let's look at these five areas a bit more closely.

Figure 1: The five areas of Life Balance

1. Me, Myself, and I—Being Your Best Friend

Looking at ourselves, we will see that our values, physical health, homes, financial situation and the time we give to ourselves greatly influence our Life Balance.

Probably the most distinguishing factor about you is **your values**; your purpose in life, your ethics, your spirituality—however you choose to call it. These terms all address that one part of you that is difficult to put into words, yet is so important. The meaning you see, the right that you differentiate from the wrong. I'll use the term "values" here. If you have not yet established a clear set of values for yourself and have not yet made it a part of your life to live these values, then catching up on this will significantly improve your Life Balance.

"A sound mind in a healthy body" is an oft-quoted reference to the fact that we live in a body and with this body, we seek **health**. Because many of us have to deal with challenges regarding our health, Life Balance is not strictly about being healthy, but about being in balance with the physical challenges we face. It goes without saying that this can be one of the most difficult aspects of Life Balance.

The **home** that we choose for ourselves is another important element of our Life Balance. A home provides shelter and protection as well as a place for social interaction, but it can turn into a burden if the financial or operational requirements overwhelm us or if the environment challenges us with noise, hostile neighbors or other stress factors that prevent us from recharging at home.

Being at ease with ourselves is another key prerequisite for improving our Life Balance. This requires **time that we spend on and for ourselves**. During this time, we are not catering to others, living up to expectations, or chasing the next task to be completed. This time for ourselves is needed to contemplate what's important to us, to do the things we like and to recharge after times of high activity. Making time for ourselves is an important task in life. Some need more, others need less, so determine the amount of time you need for yourself and secure it in your day, your week and your year.

Being able to balance our values, our health, our financial situation, and our home, as well as spend time on ourselves will allow us to be our strongest ally in improving our Life Balance.

2. One Plus One Equals Three?
How Important Is a Relationship for Life Balance?

Having someone walk through life with you as your partner can be an important part of your Life Balance. However, that does not mean that any partner is automatically good and no partner is always bad. As proof, you will easily find couples in your own environment who are more out of balance than singles you know. Consequently, the question is not whether or not one has a partner but rather whether one has a partner if one wants one; whether the partner is right for you and if the resulting partnership is good for both of your Life Balances.

3. Blood Is Thicker Than Water – Family Ties

We cry, we laugh, we sooth and we yell – family is interesting, emotional, and often nerve-wracking. No matter what the status though, the ties between family members are generally stronger than any other ties we weave in our lives and consequently the family ecosystem has a very strong impact on our Life Balance.

How close or far certain family members live from you and how active your communication is impacts if your family is a source of strength and support—or a source of stress and disharmony.

4. Doubling Your Joys, Dividing Your Sorrows – That's What Friends Are For!

There are phases in our lives when we find our friends are more important to us than our families. This only emphasizes the importance of our friends for our well-being. There is no optimal number of friends; neither is there the perfect mix of best, close and casual friends one should have. Some of us need one best friend, others want to be surrounded by many but not go too deep with any of them.

However, what we all need to do is to understand our needs and to make room for them so that they can be fulfilled.

5. Don't Trade In Your True Calling for a Job – Doing Work You Dislike Is Wasting Your Life

While the concept of work-life-balance misleads and narrows down a number of balance factors to only two—your Life

Balance *is* still strongly determined by your work. Work doesn't always equal going to the office every day or even pursuing a profession that pays. Work – in a broader sense – is what we spend our waking hours on; it is the change we try to make on this planet with our daily efforts. This definition of work includes people commuting to an office each morning, freelancers, artists, mothers at home, retirees engaged in a charity, athletes striving to do their best.

Obviously, a minimum degree of financial safety is necessary for good Life Balance. Often, this financial safety comes from your work. No matter what it is though, if your work does not support your purpose in life, your Life Balance will suffer on a conscious or subconscious level.

Life Balance Is Not a Destination, It Is a Journey

I hope that this explanation of Life Balance gives you a good starting point from which to examine your own Life Balance. I hope that it inspires you to investigate the five dimensions – yourself, partnership, family, friends, and work – and provides you with insight on how to enhance your Life Balance. If areas are lacking, don't be discouraged. Life Balance is a journey, not a destination. The rewards of dealing with it are plentiful and include happiness, finding your own resilience against hardships and challenges, as well as a clear glimpse of what is important in your life.

This book will be your guide on your journey so please enjoy it!

2. How to Improve Your Life Balance

As we saw in the previous chapter, Life Balance is a journey, not a destination. Let's have a look at the milestones of that journey so that you don't get lost.

Step 1: Assessing Your Current Life Balance Situation

As you can see in Figure 2 below, ideally, you begin your journey with an assessment of your current Life Balance. If you are already aware of which of the five life areas (you, your relationship, your family, your friends, your work) you want to

Figure 2: Milestones on your journey towards better Life Balance

improve, then you can skip this step. Otherwise, please refer to page 9 to find out how the mybalance Life Balance Check can help you assess your current Life Balance.

It's always wise to focus when trying to achieve something, so don't try to change your whole life at once. If you feel that you have to improve your Life Balance in several areas, pick the one area that bothers you most right now, since it will be the start in your journey towards better Life Balance.

Step 2: Picking from a Wealth of Advice

Enjoy this book and browse through the tips, recommendations, and gadgets on the following pages. There are plenty of categories and icons available to make it easy for you to find what's most relevant for you. The next chapter (see page 11) will give you some tips on how to best use this book.

Feeling out of balance and being pressed for time usually go hand-in-hand. Focus on our timesaving tips first. These are marked with our *timesaver icon*. Create some space for you to breathe, then start looking at some of the activities you want to add to your daily routine.

Chapter 1 in the resource section has a very useful tool for you: On page 226, there's a list of all the advice in this book. You can use this list to build your *Individual Life Balance Improvement Plan*.

Remember, there is no rush. You can always come back and add more items to your plan. So get started, pick the first items that appeal to you and start incorporating them into your life.

Not every tip will appeal to everyone, which is why you can also mark the tips you *don't like* in your Individual Life Balance Improvement Plan.

While some of our advice touches on serious topics, others are more tongue-in-cheek. Some tips come in the form of general advice, others direct the reader to a book or an internet link. I've also added some favorite tools and gadgets suggested by users and staff of mybalance.net for a better Life Balance.

Step 3: Daily Practice

As you add items to your Individual Life Balance Improvement Plan, make sure to reserve some time both daily and weekly to review your list. Your plan is a living document, so mark items as completed once you feel that you have mastered them and keep adding new ones that also appeal to you. Make sure you give the items you like enough time to turn from a good idea into a useful habit.

Share your plan and your intention to improve your Life Balance with the people close to you. Ask your partner or your friends to hold you accountable for something you are determined to incorporate into your life.

Ideally, keep a diary for notes on what worked well and what helped you attain better Life Balance.

And just like working out, it's always more fun to do things together. So if you can think of someone who could also do with more Life Balance, invite them to join in and make the journey with you.

Option: Become a Member at www.mybalance.net

I founded mybalance.net as a web-based resource for individual users and corporate teams who want to improve their Life Balance.

If you enjoy doing things via the Internet or joining communities online, consider becoming a member at mybalance.net. The portal is a great resource, offering a profound Life Balance self-assessment developed with leading researchers around the world.

A multipage results report will tell you exactly where you stand and all advice from this book can also be found at mybalance.net in an easy to sort and filter format. You can also build your Individual Life Balance Improvement Plan online there.

Additionally you will find resources such as a diary, a forum, a blog, and a community to vet ideas with. I personally love that you can use mybalance.net at home or on your mobile device.

Rebate Offer: Don't Pay Twice

You won't be charged twice for the same content. If you want to purchase a membership at mybalance.net, use the coupon code

BOOK-6856

to get your purchase price for this book refunded and applied towards your membership fee.

Figure 3: Check-out www.mybalance.net for an introduction video with more details on the portal

3. How to Use This Book

Live Balance Categories

By now we have learned that there are five main areas in your life to be balanced: yourself, relationship, family, friends, and work (see Figure 4). To assess your Life Balance you will want to look at all five areas and determine where you are in good shape and where you want to improve.

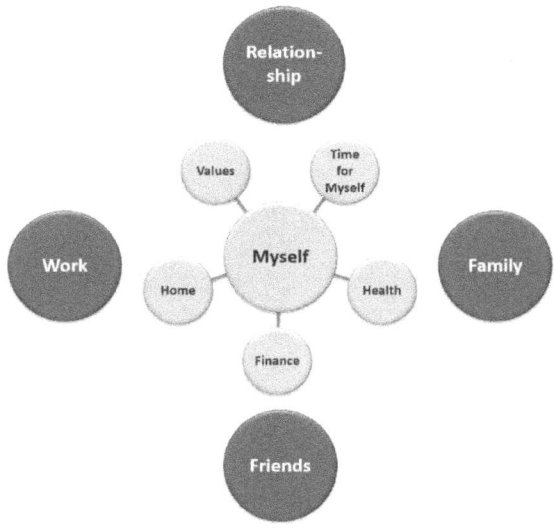

Figure 4: The five Life Balance areas

However, improvement tips and tricks for the three categories of relationship, family, and friends are very similar. All three deal with your relationship to other people. Consequently, the advice in this book is structured in three categories: myself, others, work. You can apply the advice from the *others* category towards the life areas of relationship, family, and friends (see Figure 5).

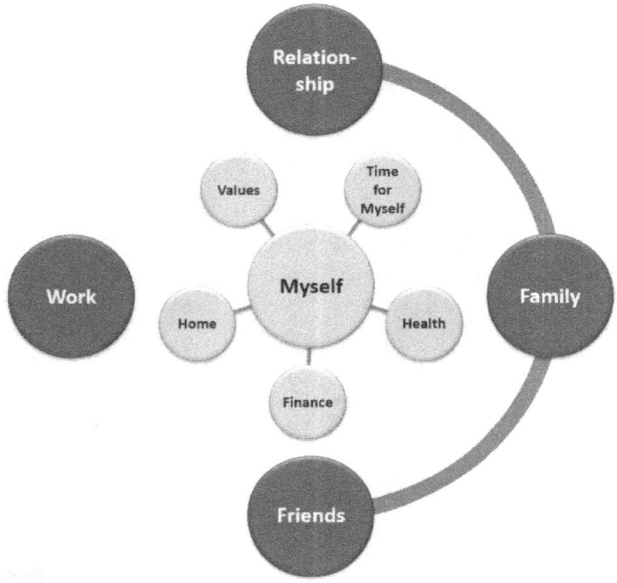

Figure 5: The three advice categories: Myself – Others - Work

Three Main Types of Advice

Each bit of advice is categorized into one of the following three groups and marked with the corresponding icon:

- Advice 👤
- Books 📕
- Gadgets 🔧

 Independent of their advice category, tips that help you free up time are marked with a ***timesaver icon***. I recommend that you look at these first to create some breathing space for yourself before you look at adding anything to your daily routine.

Life Balance Improvement Plan

The table on page 226 in the resource section of this book can become your Individual Life Balance Improvement Plan. There is a list of all the advice from this book together with three columns:

- Check the thumbs down 👎 column for those tips that you can't relate to. Remember, everyone's different, hence not every tip appeals to everyone.

- Checks the thumbs up 👍 column for those tips that seem to have potential for you. They become your Individual Life Balance Improvement Plan.

- Leave both columns free for the tips you want to consider later. Remember, there is no rush. Try to incorporate new habits one at a time and don't frustrate yourself by putting too much onto your list.

- Check the checkmark ✓ column for each tip you believe you have mastered so that you can start focusing on the other tips on your list.

A Note on Recommendations

In this book, I will sometimes recommend gadgets or tools our team has found helpful for attaining better Life Balance. These recommendations were either suggested by mybalance staff members or users. We do not accept recommendations from third parties such as manufacturers or retailers; we do not sell space for gadgets to appear on the site nor in the book, nor do we accept the unsolicited submission of product samples for any purpose.

In some cases, the book will provide a link to a product description on Amazon.com. I feel that providing these links adds valuable information with regards to product specifications, user ratings, pricing, as well as a chance to make a product comparison. By providing product links, I do not endorse Amazon.com over any comparable retailer.

However, be advised that if you choose to follow a link to Amazon.com from this book and you decide to make a purchase as a result of following that link, mybalance.net may receive a compensation from Amazon.

On Short Links

Whenever links in this book got too long to be conveniently typed into a browser, I used a link shortening service (www.bit.ly) to shorten links. This allows you to use the links from the book without undue effort or risk of mistyping.

Feedback to the Author.

If you have suggestions or any other form of feedback, you can contact me and my team via email at

team@mybalance.net

Part 2 Life Balance Advice for Yourself

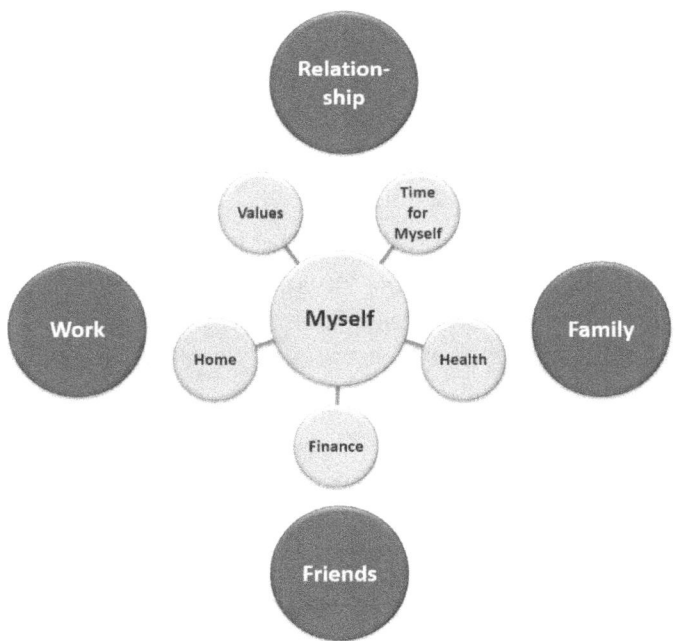

1. Find the Time

  If you've made it this far to improve your Life Balance, you've already taken a big step. Congratulations! But maybe you're already wondering how you will find the time to devote to improving your Life Balance.

In this book you will find two different kinds of advice. The first type of advice helps you free up time, so that you can utilize the second type of advice on how to spend this time on a more joyful life, leading to better Life Balance.

How Busy Are You Really?

When you listen to yourself, your friends and your colleagues talk about being busy, the situation can seem grim. Everyone seems to be working twelve hour days, sleeping six hour nights, and still not have the time to finish what they want. The good news is that we usually overestimate the amount of time we spend on daily activities.

Check out the American Time Use Survey (bit.ly/mb-1101a) to see how many of us have a wrong perception of how we spend our time.

Unconsciously exaggerating how busy you are can ruin your mood and dampen your self-esteem throughout the day. Here are three simple steps to change your attitude towards time:

- Log your time.
- Understand your time eaters.
- Choose how to spend your time.

Logging Your Time

Start by keeping a time log for a week so that you understand how much time you actually spend on various activities. Most likely, you will find that you spend less time working, less time cleaning up after your children, less time on household chores and more time on the little Internet time eaters like Facebook, news pages, or online games. After the first few days of keeping the time log, you will start to see patterns and your individual areas where you have a wrong perception of the amount of time spent.

Understand Your Time Eaters

Once you understand your personal time patterns, you can start to see where you can spend less time and get a more realistic understanding of how busy you really are. Of course, this is not about eliminating every little Facebook break or online article read, but it is about making a conscious decision over how much time you really want to devote to these activities.

Be in Control Again

Having your time log show you how you are using your twenty-four hours puts you into the unique position of being able to choose and be in control of your time again.

You can now choose where you want to spend less and where you want to spend more of your time and you can also start to incorporate this newly won control into your language. "I don't have time for this," communicates a lack of control; "I don't want to spend time on this," means you make the conscious decision to not do something in favor of another activity. This also means that "I don't have time" ceases to be a viable excuse, so use your new-found responsibility wisely.

Throughout this book, you will find additional tips that help you free up your time. We have tagged these tips with the timesaver icon to help you search for them. As you free up more time in your days, you can choose what to do with your newly won available time.

Key Takeaways:

1. Track your time spent in a time log for a week if you find yourself complaining often about being too busy. See where your time is actually going.
2. Understand your individual time eaters and areas where you overestimate the time you spend.
3. Actively choose where you want to spend more or less time. Say "I don't want to spend time on this" instead of "I don't have time for this" to show your newly won control over your own time.

2. Do You Get Enough Tranquility?

You're busy juggling your home, work and personal life and in that shuffle tranquility may very well be the last thing on your mind, but part of having good Life Balance is recognizing the importance quiet time can have in improving the quality of your life. Social media and gadgets are giving us limitless opportunities for social interaction and stimulation, but as the speed and quantity of these exchanges increases, the quality of our experiences can drastically go down.

It pays to slow down and treat yourself to some tranquility—it's in those quiet moments that you are able to reflect, concentrate, find your inner peace, act more consciously, perceive and enjoy beauty, show compassion, and actively live each experience as it comes, rather than have it all whip by.

Here are some tips on how to slow down and get some tranquility back in your life.

1. Restrict Your Media Consumption

  a. Actively choose what and why you listen to something, instead of automatically switching on the TV or radio and living your life with a constant stream of background noise.

  b. Exercise without music for a change. Allow yourself to tune in to the sounds of nature or the sounds of the city. Let your thoughts and ideas soar.

  c. Go offline when you're on vacation, or at least limit your online time to short periods. Enjoy the offline joys and give them as much room as possible.

d. Focus on the company around you when you're at a dinner or a party—your friends, family and new acquaintances. Resist the urge to constantly check your pinging smart phone or review Facebook. Better yet, turn your phone off.

e. Live an experience fully—not behind a small screen. It's fun to share experiences or milestones on Instagram or Facebook, but if you're staring at your child's recital through a small screen the entire time, you are missing out. Actively perceiving and enjoying the experience is more important than sharing it on a social media site.

2. Actively Seek Tranquility

a. Make it a part of your routine in the mornings. Take some deep breaths by the window or have a contemplative cup of coffee before rushing off.

b. Spend a quiet moment at night before you go to sleep. Reflect on your day and think about the next one. Choose a calming thought for the night. Page 69 has a great book recommendation just for that.

c. Try mediation to create calm periods during your week that allow you to get in tune with yourself and your values. You can find an *Introduction to Meditation* on page 32.

d. Make your conversations more profound. Listen, think about what was said, react to it internally – only then add your next bit to the conversation.

e. Make room for deep conversations. Choose an evening with the TV off for time to discuss the less urgent, but more important topics in life. Choose meeting formats with friends that cater to good conversations, e.g. hiking or walking instead of going to the movies.

f. De-clutter your calendar. If you don't like going to an event or don't draw energy from it, cancel it. Make time for what is really important to you.

3. Act More Consciously

   a. Live the very moment of now. Eat consciously and enjoy your meal; play with your children, give them your full attention and feel the energy and magic they emit.

   b. Spot the small delights: a bird singing, beautiful flowers, a funny moment that makes you smile.

   c. Treat yourself to a moment of contemplation before you react to something unpleasant. Think it over or—better yet—sleep on it and enjoy how much more relaxed and appropriate your reply will be.

If you're feeling hurried and rushed, there are things you can do to slow your life down and reclaim some serenity. Decrease your time with gadgets and social media platforms; increase quality time with friends and time with yourself. Enjoy the small joys of your day: mealtimes, working out, meeting with friends, playing with pets, having an outing with your kids, spotting something beautiful, having a meaningful conversation. It is these small points of color that make up the big picture and more moments of tranquility mean a more satisfying Life Balance.

Key Takeaways:

1. Restrict your media consumption – actively choose what and why you listen to or watch something.

2. Actively seek tranquility – make it part of your everyday routine.

3. Act more consciously – live now, enjoy the small delights, and contemplate before you react to something unpleasant.

3. Important Things First

  The situation is familiar: you know what you should be doing, but you are so tired you end up doing nothing. Or your task list overwhelms you and you waste time focusing on something completely irrelevant.

The first question you may have to ask yourself is what should I be doing? What is truly important right now? Once you start to think about it, obviously, not everything can be a top priority. Some tasks should be done immediately, not because they are urgent, but simply to get them out of the way and some tasks can be combined to save time. It seems counterproductive, but sometimes stopping your work to take some time out is the exact thing you need to get yourself back on track. Consider the following tips:

Power Nap

Sleep deprivation and fatigue are major causes of lack of focus and inefficiency, which is why some companies are finally allowing employees to rejuvenate with a fifteen minute nap. It does not have to be long. A ten to twenty minute nap is enough to freshen you up and get you ready to face the rest of your day. If it is at all in your power to do so, make your nap a priority—any work that follows will be done with more clarity and drive.

Good Weather

It seems straight-forward, but if the weather is nice, make it a priority to go outside and use it! Not enough exposure to sun and general lack of outdoor activities have been clearly linked to depression and anxiety, especially in areas with long winters, or frequent rain. Enjoying an afternoon out with family and friends or even taking a walk in the sun on your lunch break is an excellent way to get movement, socialize, and get some balance back into your life.

The Two Minute Rule

Sending a one-line email reply. Taking out the trash. How many times have you put off something that would have taken literally moments, only to find a horde of tiny tasks waiting for you later? GTD (Getting Things Done) guru David Allen has a great rule to combat this problem. Ask yourself: can the task be completed in two minutes or less? If the answer is yes do it right away and keep those micro-tasks from overwhelming you later.

They Say Don't Multitask, But...

"I haven't talked to that person in forever..." Do you find yourself saying or thinking that about some of your family members or friends? Lack of contact is the simple cause of many friendships or family relations getting strained, which is why a headset for your phone (the chapter on page 154 speaks to that) works wonders here. The next time you're ironing, pruning your garden, washing dishes, or doing any number of household tasks that don't require too much concentration, use that time and your headset to call a friend or family member and reconnect.

At work, a boss will always tell you what you need to be doing next. At home (or if you are your own boss) It can be difficult to stay on top of tasks, so if you're feeling a little in over your head, take a moment to identify what is most important, what can be done quickly and gotten out of the way and remember that sometimes, it makes perfect sense for your Life Balance to make resting or socializing a priority.

Key Takeaways:

1. Identify what you need to be doing next and act on it, even if what you need is to take a break or to go outside.

2. Do short quick tasks quickly to avoid them piling up. Use the two minute rule.

3. Use a phone headset to reconnect with friends and family while you do chores.

4. Block Time for Important Things

  Your life makes many demands on you from many sides: your family loves to spend time with you, your job requires much time spent at work, your friends invite you to activities. On top of this are the logistics of life—laundry, fixing things at home, running errands. The list sometimes seems endless.

While all of these demands are important to address, you need to ensure you have time for yourself. Some might need more, others less but we all need time for ourselves to balance the time we give to others.

I recommend that you think about how much time you need for yourself and then make plans to secure it in your daily routine.

1. How Much Time Do You Need for Yourself?

Write down on piece of paper how much time you would like to ideally have for yourself. Go small to big. For example:

- On a daily basis I need …
    - … 30 minutes to meditate or
    - … 30 minutes to work out or
    - … 30 minutes to end the day reading my book or
    - … 30 minutes to take a walk to unwind from the day.
- On a weekly basis I need …
    - … one evening where the family doesn't count on me so that I can make spontaneous plans without having to check with anyone, or
    - … one weekend day where my partner doesn't count on me, so that I can make plans without having to

check with anyone (my partner then gets the other day), or
  - ... one afternoon where I can spend time on my hobby or
  - ... one morning where I can sleep in to recharge.
- On a yearly basis I need ...
  - ... one week where nobody relies on me and I can go places by myself/with friends/with my partner/ ... or
  - ... one week where I schedule all of my medical check-ups, because otherwise, I won't do it.

How much time is required will differ for each individual and depends on how much time you need for yourself to balance out the time you give for others. You might want to review this list every now and then, as your requirements may change over time.

2. Block Time in Your Calendar

If your life is closely linked to another person's life, such as your partner, roommate, or other family members etc., you'll want to discuss your list with that person to get their support. That other person may find that they have similar requests and the resulting agreements you make can turn into improvements for the both of you.

Once you have agreed on the list—or decided it by yourself—block this time in your calendar. Do this for the whole year in advance, as you can always make changes, but if you don't block time for what's important in your life well in advance, then it most likely won't happen.

You might not actually use every blocked time slot in your calendar, but foregoing it is much better than needing it and not having blocked time for it.

Key Takeaways:

1. Acknowledge that you need time for yourself to balance all the time you give to others.

2. Determine how much time you need for yourself on a daily, weekly, and yearly basis.

3. Block this time in your calendar to ensure it is available when you need it. Make sure to make good use of the time once you have blocked it.

5. Shut Up Your Gadgets

 Affectionately, we call them gadgets—they're our little electronic helpers here to make life easy for us and we surround ourselves with as many as we can. Unfortunately, this tendency has led to gadgets becoming increasingly invasive and entering situations in our life where they do not belong.

Examine an average work day and you'll find that frequent distractions are a main reason for less than optimal productivity. Email clients, chat programs, news readers, social networks are all emitting non-stop signals causing distraction and procrastination; and it's gadgets that provide more constant access to these signals than ever before.

Here are the ten best tips on how to increase your productivity by shielding yourself from distractions:

1. Reduce the flood of information you are following. How many newsfeeds, information pages, and newsletters do you really need? Frequently weeding out the ones that are less interesting for you will help you manage information overflow and reduce unnecessary notifications and updates.

2. If you have implemented my suggested way of doing email (see page 182), you'll have a folder in your email strictly for CC-ed messages. Direct your newsletters and newsfeeds via email to this folder and keep your main inbox for your most important messages.

3. Don't multitask! It is scientifically proven that multitasking is highly inefficient at best, impossible at worst, so either

consume new information or focus on your work, but don't do both at the same time.

4. Dedicate a certain time of your day (or two or three smaller periods) to processing email and avoid processing each individual message as it comes in. You will be pleased to see that by dealing with them in batches, a number of emails will have already been resolved and not requiring your input by the time you get to them.

5. Switch off notifications for incoming email on your computer and your mobile device. Since you have dedicated times during the day to attend to your email, you don't need notifications anymore. This will reduce distraction for you and also for people around you. Another benefit of switching off new email notifications on your computer is that they can be disturbing, indiscreet, or embarrassing when they pop up while you present using your PC.

6. Cut your online time in half! Some people might be online for ten to twelve hours each day, or what we call "constantly connected." While this may seem like a grand technological achievement, it severely limits you in what you can achieve in the off-line world. Think about how you can reduce your online time per day by fifty or more percent. Imagine what this would do to the quality of your work and the relationships you have with your friends and family.

7. When you start a new project or want to develop something new and innovative, consider moving away from your PC or switching it off. Develop your ideas on paper to avoid distraction. Only use your gadgets again once the concept is finalized.

8. As tempting as it may be, stay away from your social networks during work. They are major time wasters.

9. Do not be constantly available. By switching off your devices during times of silence, sleep, personal activities, or family time you protect the quality of these periods. It is all right to establish set periods where others can't reach you. Remember, if somebody disturbs you with a call on your cell phone, it is your fault, not theirs. Think about times when you should or could switch off your phone and make this a habit in your life. Unless you are working in a profession that requires you to be on-call twenty-four hours, others (clients as well as friends) will learn to respect limited availability once you establish it. On the other hand, if you establish that you can be reached under any circumstance, at any hour, for any trivial reason—others will take advantage of that as well.

10. Differentiate between private and work communication. Set up your gadgets in a way that allows you to switch off private communication while you are at work and vice versa. Treating yourself to truly work-free evenings and weekends will allow you to focus more intently when you are at work.

Key Takeaways:

1. Understand that for all their convenience, gadgets do present drawbacks. Be aware of them.

2. Limit the time where you are available for everyone. Limit your time online and do not try to multitask.

3. Separate work and private communication in your gadgets as well as in your calendar.

6. Introduction to Meditation

Part 1 – The Benefits

 You may have friends who meditate, you may have felt a desire in the past to just stop and enjoy some silence. You may have seen meditation practiced in a movie or have read about it and have felt an attraction or curiosity towards it. Whatever your first exposure to this ancient practice was, meditation has a lot to offer in terms of relaxation and focus and it is worth trying out.

Two Myths

Before I start, let's do away with two myths about meditation.

1. *Meditation is thinking about absolutely nothing.* The origin of this misunderstanding might stem from a wrong translation. Ancient yoga schools have always described meditation as finding the silence between two thoughts and while this is a difficult concept to translate, it does not boil down to having an absolutely empty mind, which may be impossible to achieve. Instead, it is about not being attached to a thought and letting it pass, and finding the increasing breaks between one thought and the next.

2. *You need to be a Buddhist to meditate.* While you can find meditation in most world religions including Buddhism, the essence of meditation is about contemplation and withdrawing from external disturbances so that you may focus on the inside. Here I want to look at meditation independent from religion, to explore it as a state that helps us find spiritual development and time to think in our daily life.

The Benefits of Meditation

More than ever, meditation can help you make the right decisions and think more clearly. Too many of our decisions are made subconsciously. Many of us spend time wondering why we are unsatisfied in our lives: why are we unhappy at work, what went wrong in our relationship, how did that accident happen? Much of this has to do with making day to day decisions unconsciously, without considering the thoughts and emotions within us. Taking the time to examine these thoughts and emotions with some distance will help us make better decisions and that is what meditation is about.

No special equipment, places or rituals are necessary. You don't need special clothes, or to sit in the lotus position—in fact, you can meditate on your commuter train, in your gym, on a hike—you name it.

The six basic elements you will need to explore this beneficial practice are: **posture, grounding, breathing, massage, music** and **guiding**.

Key Takeaways:

1. Create time to reflect in your daily routine.
2. Explore meditation as a practice to ground yourself and find access to your inner values.
3. Be patient and try different ways to meditate, relax, recharge or better process the complexities of the day.

Part 2 – Posture and Grounding

 ### Do I Need to Sit in the Lotus Position?

In the Far East, meditation is about bringing your spirit, your soul, and your body into unison. Some yoga schools require certain postures, others don't. For our purposes here, there are no special rules on how to sit or lay during meditation. Remember though that while a nap is always good, it has nothing to do with meditation. If you chose to lie down, make sure you don't fall asleep. You should be in a comfortable position, sitting or reclining straight. As long as you're not slouching, it doesn't matter if you sit comfortably, walk around, go on a hike or lay down. How you approach your meditation is up to you.

Grounding – Helping Weather the Storms of Life

For our purposes, we will not look at transcendental meditation, which is about leaving your life behind and ascending to higher spheres. Since we want to stay here and maintain the unity of our current body and mind, grounding is very important for our exercise.

(Disclaimer: Try the physical portions of this chapter only if you are physically in good shape. If you feel discomfort or pain, stop immediately. When in doubt, talk to your physician before trying any of the exercises described in this chapter.)

Feel the planet beneath you with this exercise:

- Stand comfortably with your feet shoulder width apart.

- Bend your knees slightly and feel your weight on your heels.

- Close your eyes if it's comfortable.

- Now imagine you are a tree. Feel your roots going deep, feel your crown high in the wind.
- Bend forward, backward, and sideways to the left and the right and feel your weight get distributed on all parts of the soles of your feet.
- Feel the ground through your feet. Feel how grounded you are. Feel how you stand on this planet, rotating and circling around the sun. Feel the gravity holding you.

Now, open your eyes.

- Slowly start walking in place and increase your speed until you are at a slow jog.
- Roll your weight across your feet from heel to ball to toes.
- Feel the floor or ground beneath you.
- As you get your grounding, make a note to yourself to try this the next time you walk down the street or hike through a forest.

You can also try grounding while sitting down.

- Find a comfortable position. You can use a pillow or a little block to sit on or anything that makes you feel comfortable.
- Close your eyes and feel the grounding through your bottom, your legs, your feet and any part of you that touches the floor. Concentrate on these areas where you touch the floor.
- Loosen your shoulders, feel how your weight concentrates in your pelvis. Feel how your upper body seems almost weightless and levitates.
- Feel the planet under you and breathe deeply. Imagine your roots going deep through the floor and into the earth.

Without opening your eyes, shift into a reclining position.

- Move slowly and feel each movement as you make it.
- Stretch your legs, relax your face, including your forehead.
- Breathe normally.
- Now let yourself sink into the floor by imagining you are falling from the sky in this horizontal relaxed position.

When you are done, roll to one side and come back to a sitting position. Open your eyes. Did you feel your grounding?

This simple grounding exercise is something you can take a few moments to practice every day to have a short break of relaxation and peace. As you explore your own individual way to meditate, you'll discover different postures and ways of grounding yourself.

Key Takeaways:

1. Don't be too formal about your meditation; you can meditate while you sit, lay down or even walk or hike.

2. Ground yourself during your meditation to maintain the unity of your body and mind.

3. Try some of the grounding exercises to find the energy coming from the earth beneath your feet.

Part 3 – Breathing

What's So Special about Breathing?

 The next element of meditation is breathing. While it sounds simple, the breathing I speak about here is different from the breathing we do throughout the day.

There are different kinds of breathing for different purposes in meditation. If we want to concentrate, we can apply yoga breathing and Ujaya breathing. For relaxing, or to fight insomnia, we can use alternate nostril breathing (also referred to as *moon and sun* breathing). If we want to mobilize energy within us for an important task ahead, we can apply a technique called the breath of fire.

a)   Yoga Breathing for Concentration

Yoga breathing–also referred to as long deep breathing–aims at reaching a steady harmony between inhaling and exhaling. Try to spend at least three seconds on each inhalation and three seconds on each exhalation. Once you feel more comfortable with this breathing technique, you will easily be able to spend four to eight seconds on each breath and relax through your yoga breathing.

Inhale through your nose. On the inhale, actively push your belly out. Open your chest and fill your chest cavity up with air; fill up your diaphragm. Keep your shoulders broad, your chest and ribcage open and feel the air flow into your lungs.

On the exhale, push the air out of your diaphragm and feel your stomach slowly suck in, but keep your chest open and your shoulders broad. You can exhale through your mouth if you like.

Try this for a few minutes for increased focus and concentration.

b) *Ujaya Breathing for Energy*

Called *victorious* breathing, Ujaya breathing helps mobilize your energy and wake you up. Once used to prep warriors for battle, use it before going on stage for a presentation, going into the conference room for a difficult meeting or before meeting with your boss for an important conversation.

Ujaya breathing works like yoga breathing, but it requires that you narrow your throat and activate your vocal cords. Keep your mouth closed, but make the same hissing noises as if you were breathing against a mirror. The force you put into your breathing will activate the energy boost you need.

Use this technique if you're feeling lethargic at the office or need a burst of energy but don't use it if you're trying to relax or fall asleep. For that, try the technique below.

c) *Alternate Nostril Breathing for Relaxation*

The alternate nostril breathing technique is also referred to as moon and sun breathing and it is particularly useful right before meditation or before going to bed.

To start, move your hand towards your face and hold your nose with your thumb and your ring finger. Put your middle finger and your index finger where your "third eye" is—onto the spot between your eyebrows.

Now close one nostril with your thumb and inhale. Then let go and close your other nostril with your middle finger and exhale. Inhale with the same nostril and then switch back to closing your nostril with your thumb and exhale. Close your eyes as you do this and enjoy the soothing and calming effect of this alternating breathing. Make sure you inhale as long as you exhale.

A special version of the alternate nostril breathing technique is moon breathing. This will help you when you're having trouble falling asleep. For moon breathing, use only your left nostril to inhale and your right one to exhale.

Sun breathing will help you relax after you wake up in the morning. It is the opposite of moon breathing, i.e. use only your right nostril to inhale and your left one to exhale.

d)   *The Breath of Fire for Power*

Another power boosting breathing technique is the breath of fire. Don't use it before meditation or sleep, but use it in place of a cup of coffee or whenever you need to activate your energy stores.

The breath of fire works like this:

Take a very deep breath. Then–with your mouth opened just a little bit –blow the air out in ten to twenty short puffs before you slowly inhale again. Actively tighten your stomach (your diaphragm) as you exhale. Repeat this a few times and you will feel the energy boost.

Key Takeaways:

1. Explore how the different kinds of yoga breathing can either energize or calm you.

2. Think about where this effect can be helpful for you at work, during your workout or elsewhere.

3. Start your day with a short breathing exercise ... and end it with one too.

Part 4 – Surrounding Conditions

Acupressure and Massage–How Do You 'Feel' Today?

 Our next important ingredient to meditation involves scalp massage. Touching the crown of your head or massaging your neck will help you relax before you meditate.

Try this by moving your right hand onto the crown of your head. Feel the warmth and caress your head like you would stroke a pet or a small child. Move your other hand to the back of your head and start to massage your neck while bending your head slightly forward.

Another technique to massage your head is using your index and middle fingers to massage the spot referred to as the third eye between your eyebrows. Feel yourself relax as you carefully rotate your fingertips in that spot with your eyes closed and your breath steady.

Use the same two fingers of both hands to massage your temples and feel how the rotating movement relaxes your forehead, your jaws, your scalp, and the rest of your head.

Using these massage techniques will help you synchronize your body, spirit, and soul in preparation for your meditation.

Music or Silence–The iPod Version of Meditation?

Whether you listen to music during your meditation or meditate in silence is up to you. While music can help you relax, you may find dealing with your MP3 player and finding the right volume distracting.

To explore meditation with music, here are some links to playlists with meditation music:

bit.ly/mb-1109b and bit.ly/mb-1109e

Guided Meditation or Silence–Start With Some Help?

During a guided meditation, a meditation trainer talks you through your experience. The comments given by your meditation trainer can take you on a mental journey or simply give you advice on how to breathe and relax. If you don't have much experience, you might like to try some guided meditation sessions. Once you develop your own routine, you can continue to meditate with the guide, or switch to your preferred music or silence.

Here are a few links to guided meditations you can try.

bit.ly/mb-1109c and bit.ly/mb-1109d

As you can see, varying posture, grounding, breathing, massage, music, and guided meditations gives you limitless varieties in your meditation practice. Explore your options and find what meditations and which environments work best for you.

A common question is whether one should meditate with eyes open or closed. While you may find it easier to meditate with your eyes closed in the beginning, ultimately, you want to be able to do it with your eyes open. One of the most famous practitioners of meditation, the Buddha, was said to always meditate with his eyes open.

If you are still unsure and don't know where to start, consider finding a meditation class in your neighborhood and start there.

Hopefully meditation will become a regular source of energy and insight in your life. Good luck!

A Word of Thanks

This introduction to meditation has been made possible through the friendly cooperation of Atalay Baysal, who has been my meditation coach for many years.

Key Takeaways:

1. See what works best for you: meditating in silence or with music—or both, depending on your mood.
2. Try a guided meditation and see if you like that better than meditating at your own pace.
3. If you like what you saw about meditation so far, consider taking a class at a yoga center nearby or signing up for a meditation retreat.

7. Working from Home Is Not Easy

While it sounds like a wonderful thing to do, working from home comes with its own challenges. Let's focus on the items related to your home— you will find more on this topic in our work section.

- Ensure that you have as much physical separation between your work area and the rest of your home as possible. You will want to maintain a separation from working hours and free time, even if you work from home. If your working area bleeds into the living space of your home, you run the risk of not being able to switch off and enjoy when you are off work.

- Distance yourself from the amenities of your home while working. Your sofa is comfortable, your gaming console is fun and your household is full of chores waiting to be done. Be disciplined in how you organize your work day. Identify your main distractors and define taboo times during which you ban them from your work day. Reward yourself during your breaks, but be your own strict boss in keeping a schedule.

- Distance yourself from the duties of work while you're off work. The laptop is still humming, the incoming email is still pinging (switch that off!), and there is that one thing that you could finish while something else is happening at home. If you want to balance your work and personal life in the same building, you'll need to be disciplined with smart rules and distinct boundaries. The time your kids brush their teeth is not the time for yet another email. It is time for fun and sharing about your day. Family dinner does not mean that email gets checked on your phone instead of on your computer; it means that you don't check email at all.

Key Takeaways:

1. Create a physical separation between your work area and the rest of your home

2. Distance yourself from the amenities of your home while you work.

3. Distance yourself from the duties of work while you're not working.

8. 1,000 Places to See Before You Die

When to Read It

While not particularly a bucket list for things to visit before you die, "1,000 Places" is a great source of ideas for your next travel adventure. If you travel a lot for business, make sure to check out your destinations in the book to get great ideas for what to squeeze in while you're there. You might also want to look up your part of the world to gain a whole new appreciation for travel gems in your neighborhood. And since I promote the idea of taking time to travel with your friends and family, this book serves as a great starting point to pick a destination.

What I Liked About It

The world's bestselling travel book, "1,000 Places" reinvented the idea of a travel book as both a wish list and a practical guide. In the words of Newsweek, it "tells you what's beautiful, what's fun, and what's just unforgettable— everywhere on Earth."

Though this book doesn't replace a detailed tour guide once you arrive to a particular destination, most entries include suggestions for places to stay, restaurants to visit, and festivals to check out. The world is calling. Time to answer!

The Details

"1,000 Places to See Before You Die" by Patricia Schultz.

Amazon link

bit.ly/mb-1112

Three things to get out of this book:

1. A wonderful itchy feeling and wanderlust while browsing for your next potential destination.

2. Great ideas on what sights to squeeze in during your next business trip.

3. Potentially, a whole new appreciation for travel gems in your vicinity.

9. Workout Music in Style

 Many of us like to listen to music when we run, walk, or work out. The movement of the head during the workout combined with sweat can make it difficult for standard earbuds to not constantly fall out, which is why I loved the Creative Aurvana Active Clip Earphones for their tight fit and great sound quality.

How It Improves Your Life Balance

Working out is a nice way to use time for yourself, and it's great for your health. If there are any gadgets that motivate you to get out there more, I am all for it.

More Cool Things

- The earphones come with a leather pouch for storage.
- The tight fit of the earphones provides a steady stream of sound without any pressure pain in the ear.
- The earphones nicely complement the Apple iPod Nano, the MP3 player I recommend for working out. While there might be better or cheaper players out there, I'm a big fan of staying within the one product family—in this case iPods, iPhones, and iPads.

Amazon Link

bit.ly/mb-1113a and bit.ly/mb-1113b

Use it to:

Listen to music on the go without losing your earphones.

10. Stop Wasting Time at Your PC

  Time spent on the Internet does not flow like regular time. Just about anyone whose job requires regular work on a PC is familiar with the dangers of a little web surfing, a little Facebook checking, a little blog browsing between tasks. RescueTime is a neat online service that lets you keep track of just how much time you spend doing what online. If your jaunts on the web are jeopardizing your productivity or if you'd like a better grasp on where the time goes, check out RescueTime.

How It Improves Your Life Balance

RescueTime is an online service that offers its users two packages. One package is completely free and can be used to track online activity and set productivity goals. The other costs around $6/month (paid by the year) and offers the user more options for tracking time spent on and offline. It also includes a very handy function for blocking time-sucking websites (or options to block certain sites during certain times of the day, or to block them after a certain period of time spent on them).

More Cool Things

- Set alerts to let yourself know when you've spent a certain amount of time on a certain site.

- Weekly email reports give you an accurate description of how you spend your time.

- Turn the function on or off, as you wish.

To try RescueTime for yourself, go to this link:
www.rescuetime.com

Use it to:

1. Be aware of the little things that waste time without benefit during your day.

2. If you run a risk of constantly getting distracted while working on your computer, try this to keep you on track.

3. Try the free version first to see if it meets your needs and actually helps you.

11. Remote Troubleshoots

  If you've got a knack for computers, you've probably had your fair share of help requests from family and friends. And you've probably gone through the hassle of trying to troubleshoot someone's PC problem over the phone.

If you're bad with computers, you probably rely on a friend or a family member for help with your computer problems. Do you feel guilty when that person has to drive across town to help you? Or do your problems have to wait until that person is in town again?

It's a common enough complaint, which is why I love TeamViewer, a software that, via Internet, allows you to completely control a computer as if you were sitting in front of it.

How It Improves Your Life Balance

With TeamViewer you can help your friends and family without the time it takes to get to them.

More Cool Things

- The software is free of charge for private use.

- There are versions for your mobile and tablet that allow you to help your friends even when you're on the go.

- In our tests, the average session to help a friend or family member took less than one third of the time it took to explain each step over the phone.

Link

www.TeamViewer.com

Use it to:

1. Help your friends and family remotely who rely on your help with their computers.

2. Get help from a friend or family member without having to follow their directions over the phone.

3. Accessing or controlling your own computer with another device from afar.

12. Values, Ethics, Faith, Religion

Which Are Right For You?

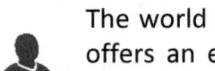

The world of good or bad, right or wrong, true or false offers an endless combination of spiritual foundations on which we may base our lives. From agnostic to fanatic, the spectrum is broad and the amount of energy that our system of beliefs can create is infinite. While you may have a more or less concrete understanding of your system of beliefs, there are four building blocks that help determine how your system of beliefs contributes to your Life Balance.

Values - Your View of What Is Right and Wrong

Values are your individual understanding of right and wrong. They help you make decisions and guide your path through life. Your values may include being honest, reliable, compassionate, or hard-working, etc. Whatever your values, they are the foundation for how you live and achieve balance.

Ethics - Your Environment's View of What Is Right and Wrong

Ethics define the set of rights and wrongs for a group of individuals; a church, a company or a nation. Ethics can be similar to values, however, your personal values can be identical or different from the ethics of the groups you belong to. As an example, you can be a vegetarian in a society with many steak houses. Or you can be against abortion in a country where it is legal.

Faith - Your View of What Is True and False

Faith describes what you believe to be true or false. Usually, faith will include a view on whether or not there is a higher being, what happens to us after we die or what the rewards or ramifications are for good or bad behavior.

Religion - An (Optional) Framework for Your Faith

Religions are a very well defined set of ethics and faith combined with rules and organizational structures. The world's largest religions are Christianity, Islam, Hinduism and Buddhism.

How Much Is About You?

Your Life Balance is affected by all four of these dimensions. Roughly speaking, values and faith are about you, whereas ethics and religion are about others. Your values may or may not match the ethics of the groups to which you belong. Your faith can make you a member of a religion or exist outside of organized religion.

You will have values, whether you are aware for them or not. If you don't spend some time reflecting on your values, you risk missing out on a key guiding factor in your life and may be left without a sense of direction or purpose. If you have experienced these feelings, consider reflecting more on your values and on how you live up to them. Thinking about your values can happen during your commute to work, on a peaceful walk in the forest or whenever you see fit. You can also consider adding meditation to your daily or weekly routine to give you more time to get in touch with your system of beliefs.

Your faith does not necessarily include a traditional belief in God. Rather, your belief in the existence or non-existence of a higher being, your understanding of the events after your death, and view of the effects of "good" and "bad" are among the key elements of your faith. If your faith is in line with a religion, then you might be a member of a church. Otherwise, your faith may be a very personal and private matter for you.

Stay in Touch with Your Inner Truths

Whatever your values and faith, make sure you give yourself enough time to be in touch with both and let them play an active part of your Life Balance. Understanding your values and faith will allow you to make life decisions much more easily. They will let you walk your own path and put you more in control of your life.

The Dalai Lama said it well:

"Those who have little interest in spirituality shouldn't think that human inner values don't apply to you. The inner peace of an alert and calm mind are the source of real happiness and good health. Our human intelligence tells us which of our emotions are positive and helpful and which are damaging and to be restrained or avoided."

Key Takeaways:

1. Be clear about your values and your faith.

2. Understand how much or how little they comply with the ethics and the religions in your society.

3. Make time in your life to stay in touch with your values and your faith.

13. Too Much Suffering in the World?

How Can You Be Happy with All the Suffering in the World?

Do you ever feel concerned or depressed about the amount of suffering in the world? Do you love someone whose problems cause you worry? It is a fact of life that there is pain, suffering, and misery wherever we look. All world religions acknowledge this and require their believers to keep this suffering in mind. But what is an ethical and responsible way to respond to the suffering of others while pursuing your own joy in life?

Feeling Sorrow vs. Feeling Compassion

Whether they're close to us or total strangers, when we respond to others' suffering by falling into a state of *sorrow*, what we are basically doing is doubling the suffering. We worsen our own position and possibly even the other person's position, because if we start suffering for them, they might become concerned for us or feel the urge to comfort us, hence increasing their own worries.

A straightforward example of this is a mother who cuts her finger while skinning potatoes. As she cries out in pain, her small daughter who saw the incident starts crying out of commiseration with her mother. Now the mother not only has to stop her own bleeding and bandage her finger, she also has to comfort her daughter and deal with her pain as well.

It is possible to show *compassion* for someone's pain or suffering without falling into a state of sorrow yourself. Compassion for someone else's suffering means showing support. It means putting yourself into the other person's shoes and imagining how they feel. Yet, it also means maintaining an emotional distance necessary for good advice and effective aid. In our example above, the husband who might have witnessed the mother's accident too can show his compassion by quickly grabbing a tissue and handing it to his wife and then holding her and comforting her. By this, he shows his understanding of the pain she feels while keeping calm. After that he can go and get her a bandage and maybe later during the day smile with her about the incident over a nice glass of wine.

There Is No Limit to Compassion

The example is trivial, but it shows the difference between feeling what the other person is feeling (pain/sorrow) and feeling with them, but maintaining your distance (compassion). Don't feel obliged to feel miserable when you encounter sadness or misery. You don't help those who suffer, only weaken your own ability to enjoy life. Most of all, when you become sad or depressed because someone you love is suffering, you involuntarily shift the focus of the pain from them to you—because you feel guilty or depressed, they may feel obliged to comfort you or to keep their problems to themselves in the future, adding an extra burden to their suffering.

Instead of getting depressed, practice compassion. While there is a limit to the sorrow you can endure before you collapse yourself, compassion can be limitless. Pain and sorrow will paralyze you, but compassion allows you to feel for those who suffer and at the same time be grateful for your own more fortunate situation. It helps you maintain a clear mind to provide help where it is needed.

Key Takeaways:

1. Think of a person you care about who may be currently suffering. Think about how you react to their unfortunate situation. Do you find yourself feeling depressed or guilty for your better fortune? Does this reaction help their situation and/or improve the unfortunate person's mood?

2. Try to shift your attitude. Instead of becoming sad and depressed, try to feel for them without feeling the need to push yourself into what they are feeling. This will open you up to a calmer mindset, a readiness to provide help and support, as well as grant you permission to still enjoy your own life.

3. Experience how you can offer limitless compassion where–in the past–you might have felt drained by feelings of sorrow. Don't shift the focus of pain to yourself by falling into negative thoughts.

14. Are You Two Kinds of Happy?

 The other day, I had an interesting discussion with a dear friend about the main goal in life. My friend claimed our main goal in life should be achieving good health and being healthy. Knowing many people who will never be able to achieve good health and yet remain perfectly happy individuals, I couldn't agree.

As the discussion continued, my friend and I ended up debating the value of happiness as a goal in general. My friend claimed that happiness in and of itself cannot be a goal, because it cannot be sustained. It is short-lived, and linked to unpredictable events that can end soon. Her theory was that if you made happiness your life's aim, you would get into a frenzy of hunting for pleasure after pleasure, leaving you ultimately empty and unfulfilled.

I'm glad we had this discussion, because it gave me some great insights and made me consider the nature of happiness. I came to the conclusion that the true masters of living a happy life understand that there are actually two kinds of happiness that complement each other. They need to be in balance to create a sustainable level of overall happiness in our life.

The First Kind of Happiness Is Joy

I believe what my friend had in mind when she spoke about happiness was that wonderful form of elation I would call *joy*. It is an immediate, event-based happiness that comes from enjoying a good meal, a walk in the sun, or a ride on a roller coaster. It makes us laugh and think "I love what I'm doing right now!"

The wonderful thing about joy is the euphoric feeling it can give us. That joy can come from human interactions like spending time with our family or friends. It can stem from sensual pleasures and doing fun things. However, I agree with my friend: joy in itself has some severe limitations. First, it can only happen in the absence of problems or as a distraction to our problems. An unpleasant situation at work can spoil our vacation; a struggle we have with one friend can ruin the time we have with others. Secondly, joy is usually short-lived. It is attached to an event and generally ends shortly after the event comes to an end, or can even turn into the opposite. We've all experienced post vacation blues when it was time to go back to the office, or that particularly lonely period after times of intensive interaction with our friends or family.

Joy is crucial for adding spots of color to our days, months or years, but it cannot give us enough happiness to push us through tough times, let alone serve as our primary goal in life. Luckily, there's something more.

The Second Kind of Happiness Is Fulfillment

Truly happy people compliment joy with appreciative, insight-based *fulfillment*. This feeling is longer lived and, ideally, lasts forever. It makes us say "I love what I have achieved in my life!". This happiness is based on the wisdom we have collected throughout our experiences. It draws sustainable satisfaction from the human relationships we have, the lessons we have learned, and from our resilience. Different from joy, this happiness doesn't rely on the absence of problems. Instead, it thrives on putting the problems we have into context. Challenges at work seem small when compared to what we have achieved for our company in the past. The struggle with one friend dwarfs next to the many great relationships we have. Additionally, while joy is usually self-centered and about the good things that happen to ourselves, fulfillment is more universal and appreciates the good things that happen to us, the people we care about, and mankind in general.

Joy	Fulfillment
Event-based	Appreciative, insight-based
Euphoric	Grateful
Laughter	Smiles
Shorter-lived	Longer-lived
Ends shortly after the related event	Lasts (ideally) permanently
Volatile – can result in the opposite	Sustainable
"I love what I'm doing right now!"	"I love what I have achieved in my life!"
Human interaction	Human relationships
Sensual pleasures	Resilience and satisfaction
Doing things	Knowing things
Preferences	Wisdom
Based on the absence (or forgetting) of problems	Based on putting problems into context.

Table 1: Comparing the two kinds of happiness

Fulfillment based on appreciation and insight is highly desirable and a wonderful ultimate goal in life, but the small joys are great for giving you a short-term boost and bringing the best out of your days.

When you strive for better Life Balance, remember both types of happiness.

Key Takeaways:

1. Think of some joy-based as opposed to fulfillment-based happiness you have in your life.

2. Do you feel like both are well-balanced?

3. If not, which type of happiness could be increased?

15. Look Up for Motivation

 No matter how good you are at something or where you are in life, there will always be someone higher than you and someone below. Even seemingly perfect couples fight sometimes and even a lauded expert can make a mistake. It is tempting to feel smug when we see someone messing up, so to improve your Life Balance, ask yourself, do you tend to look up to motivate yourself—or do you spend more time looking down?

Many reality shows capitalize on the looking down model. They introduce a bunch of hopeless contenders that make the viewer think 'sheesh, what a mess! At least I'm better than that guy.' While immediately satisfying and entertaining, looking down at people gives the distorted message that improvement is not necessary—because you are already better than someone else.

The real question though is, are you as good as you want to be? To achieve better Life Balance, don't look for the worst examples to comfort yourself or make excuses. Instead, evaluate your strengths and weaknesses, identify your goals, and focus on people who have achieved what you are striving for or for people who inspire you. These people can be characters or personalities on TV, in a certain field or industry you work in, or someone you know in real life.

You As a Person

Try to have at least one friend who is overall aligned with your values and who motivates you simply in how they live their life. Use them as your yardstick, instead of feeling smug about friends who are struggling.

Relationships

Don't pat yourself on the back because the neighbors are getting a divorce and you're still with your partner. Focus instead on harmonious, fun relationships that can help you improve any problems you and your partner have.

Family

Shows like "Super Nanny" can reassure anyone they are not the worst parent in the world, but remind yourself that "not being the worst" is not good enough. Aspire to be the best parent you can be.

Friends

In real life or on TV, focus on the friendships that are challenging, comforting, and/or enjoyable—not the friendships filled with constant drama and staged fights.

Work

Don't pump yourself up by looking down on the loser in the other department or the manager with the horrible leadership skills. Pick someone you admire and try to emulate them.

Same for your company: don't draw energy from the tests your competitors lost to other competitors. Find the icons inside and outside of your industry and try to perform as well as they do.

Nobody is perfect and even the nicest person may feel smug or superior at times for an ego boost. Being aware of this tendency though is already a big step. On a show like "American Idol" there is always one obvious star in a mass of self-aggrandizing, untalented people. For the best Life Balance, don't be content to be slightly better than the untalented crowd. Instead, look for true idols and stars in your life or on the screen and ask yourself, how can I be more like them? Don't look down—look up.

Key Takeaways:

1. Look for characters and idols who positively motivate you instead of laughing at untalented or self-aggrandizing people.

2. "I am better than this person" allows you to be content at your current level. Ask yourself instead, "How can I be as good as that person?"

3. Pick characters or people in your life who inspire you to do better, be it as a worker, a partner, a parent, a friend, or a human being.

16. Treat People with Kindness

 When was the last time you really got angry with someone? When did you last use your words to cut that person down? Afterwards, did you feel a mix of victory and guilt, with the remorse steadily outweighing the triumph?

One easy way to prevent these feelings of guilt is treating people with kindness. It is scientifically proven that kind behavior increases our happiness. Selfless behavior makes our body produce the hormone serotonin, which eases the tension in our body and creates positive emotions.

That's not the only benefit of treating people with kindness though. If you think about your values and how you want to live your life, you'll most likely see that kind behavior aligns more with the type of person you really want to be.

Treating people with compassion helps you build better relationships with less lingering conflicts that need to be resolved. It also helps reduce the risk of making mistakes due to misunderstandings, when you start to give people the benefit of the doubt.

Treating people with kindness helps you navigate through a conflict with your morals intact. By refusing to sink to another person's level, it will not matter how ugly the situation gets or how insulting they become.

Last but not least, being kind helps you live a more peaceful life, by preventing conflicts from arising in the first place.

The concept of the oneness of all promotes that unkind behavior to others is no different from unkind behavior to ourselves. This makes particular sense if you recall the mood you were in after your last argument. Most likely, you were just as hurt and upset as the other person in that situation.

This does not promote always giving in and letting others get away with anything. However, there is a gracious way of making a point, and often, you will find that it is also the most efficient way.

Key Takeaways:

1. Use the positive energy—physically and mentally—of treating people with kindness.

2. Learn how to make your point and defend yourself in an argument without becoming angry or insulting.

3. Observe how unkind behavior to others hurts you as well and see how the same is true for kind behavior benefiting others and yourself.

17. Depolarize

We live in an increasingly polarized world, that is to say, in a place where the middle ground of certain topics disappears in favor of the two extreme points in that discussion's space. You can potentially align your personal values by countering this trend and balancing unwanted polarization.

The Rise of Polarization

Many societies are currently seeing economical polarization in their social classes. As the middle class erodes, the gap between the very rich and the very poor increases over time. There is also social polarization, or strong individual opinions about topics such as abortion, gun control, foreign policy, same-sex marriage, social welfare etc. Even regards to questions like PC or Mac; iPhone or Android, emotions can run high.

In your workspace you might see polarization between organizational levels, such as managers and employees. There might be polarization between sales and marketing, white-collar and blue-collar employees, onshore and offshore teams.

In our societies, workspaces, and in our other groups we may be spending less time understanding the commonalities and focusing more on what separates us. The reason is simple: it is much easier to position ourselves on either pole of a topic, than to acknowledge the shades of gray in the areas in-between.

Be Part of the Solution

Be part of the solution and withstand the temptation to be part of polarization by refusing to represent extreme opinions and positions on certain topics. Take the time to try to understand the middle ground and make an effort to understand the arguments of the other side. Remember the old cliché: you can't judge another person before you've walked a mile in their shoes.

Also, keep in mind always that what seems extreme to you may seem like the middle ground to the other side—and what you consider reasonable may be another person's idea of extreme! That is to say, extremists often don't consider themselves to be so. If you've written off an opposing view point as unreasonable or extreme, might it not be possible that your views are being seen by others in the same light? Are you as open minded and objective as you believe?

Remember, you need not become ambiguous or give up your opinion. Pushing back on polarization and considering other positions simply means showing more concern, empathy, and understanding for those who don't share your point of view.

Try it, and you will see how it helps you make better decisions and break down silos created in your environment by people who like to polarize.

Key Takeaways:

1. Think about instances of polarization in your environment.

2. Try to come up with arguments for the other side in questions where you stand on an extreme side of the topic. Stay aware of the fact that to the opposing side, what you consider reasonable, straight-forward or normal may be extreme and/or outrageous.

3. Become alert for situations that polarize and do your bit to resolve them.

18. The Book of Awakening

Having the Life You Want by Being Present to the Life You Have

When to Read It

 With each chapter covering roughly one page, this book makes a good read as the last thing in your day. The calm and soothing style offers a poem or thought for each day of the year, combined with a bit of wisdom to carry you through the night into the next day. Keep it on your nightstand for some before-sleep reading.

What I Liked About It

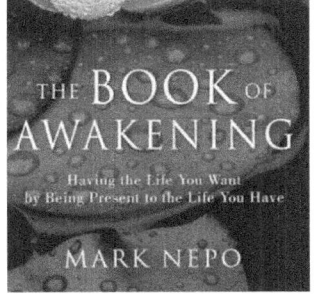

"The Book of Awakening" makes a great daily companion. Mark Nepo wrote the book more than a decade ago, in response to his journey through cancer a decade before that. The experience led him to create a daily book that anyone can benefit from.

Nepo calls it, "a book to help people meet their days and inhabit their lives. I had a commitment to create a book that could serve up inner food that could be turned to as a spiritual first-aid kit."

"The Book of Awakening" is a modern classic, speaking to the hearts of readers. It's a daily guide for living in hard times and good times, all the while reminding us that the life we're living is the life we have. Lived authentically our life can—and does—become the life we want.

The details

"The Book of Awakening: Having the Life You Want by Being Present to the Life You Have"

By Mark Nepo (Author)

Amazon link

bit.ly/mb-1207

Three things to get out of this book:

1. It can be kept on your nightstand for a great routine end to your day.
2. It offers a daily dose of wisdom.
3. It is conveniently sliced into short chapters for those who don't have much time to read.

19. The Diamond Cutter

When to Read It

 If you're thinking about your system of values and beliefs and are wondering how to apply them to your work, this book can offer you some great and entertaining examples. The first American to earn the ancient degree of *geshe*, a master of Tibetan Buddhist learning, the author lived as a monk in several Buddhist monasteries of Asia. Once he returned to the US, he was encouraged by his teacher to go back into business and test out the Buddhist principles in real life.

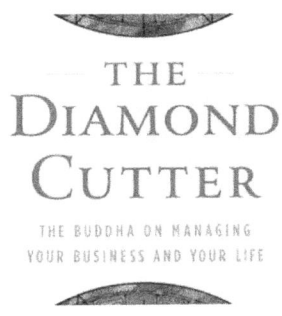

What I Liked About It

With a unique combination of ancient and contemporary Tibetan Buddhist wisdom, "The Diamond Cutter" presents readers with empowering strategies for success in their personal and professional lives.

The book is presented in three sections. The first is a translation of The Diamond Sutra, an ancient text of conversations between the Buddha and his close disciple, Subhuti. The second contains quotes from some of the best commentaries in the Tibetan Buddhist tradition. And the third main text is the practical application of Buddhist philosophies to the world of business, based upon Geshe Michael Roach's seventeen years of experience as an employee of the Andin International Diamond Corporation, a company that grew during his tenure from four employees to a world leader in the jewelry industry.

Roach's easy style and spiritual understanding make this book an invaluable source of timeless wisdom, regardless of your own familiarity with Tibetan Buddhism.

The details

"The Diamond Cutter: The Buddha on Managing Your Business and Your Life" by Geshe Michael Roach (Author) and Lama Christie McNally (Author)

Amazon link

bit.ly/mb-1208

Three things to get out of this book:

1. Great insight into how to apply your values to work.
2. An amazing story about business ethics.
3. A wonderful introduction to the principles of Tibetan Buddhism.

20. A Very Pragmatic Approach

Sometimes the rights and wrongs of life come in very pragmatic forms—like this recent Facebook posting below, which fits so well here that I wanted to share it.

Written by Regina Brett, 90 years old and first published in *The Plain Dealer* newspaper, Cleveland, Ohio.

"To celebrate growing older, I once wrote the 45 lessons life taught me. It is the most requested column I've ever written. My odometer rolled over to 90 in August, so here is the column once more:

1. Life isn't fair, but it's still good.
2. When in doubt, just take the next small step.
3. Life is too short—enjoy it.
4. Your job won't take care of you when you are sick. Your friends and family will.
5. Pay off your credit cards every month.
6. You don't have to win every argument. Stay true to yourself.
7. Cry with someone. It's more healing than crying alone.
8. It's OK to get angry with God. He can take it.
9. Save for retirement starting with your first paycheck.
10. When it comes to chocolate, resistance is futile.
11. Make peace with your past so it won't screw up the present.
12. It's OK to let your children see you cry.

13. Don't compare your life to others. You have no idea what their journey is all about.
14. If a relationship has to be a secret, you shouldn't be in it ...
15. Everything can change in the blink of an eye. But don't worry; God never blinks.
16. Take a deep breath. It calms the mind.
17. Get rid of anything that isn't useful. Clutter weighs you down in many ways.
18. Whatever doesn't kill you really does make you stronger.
19. It's never too late to be happy. But it's all up to you and no one else.
20. When it comes to going after what you love in life, don't take no for an answer.
21. Burn the candles, use the nice sheets, wear the fancy lingerie. Don't save it for a special occasion. Today is special.
22. Over prepare, then go with the flow.
23. Be eccentric now. Don't wait for old age to wear purple.
24. The most important sex organ is the brain.
25. No one is in charge of your happiness but you.
26. Frame every so-called disaster with these words 'In five years, will this matter?'
27. Always choose life.
28. Forgive but don't forget.
29. What other people think of you is none of your business.
30. Time heals almost everything. Give time time.
31. However good or bad a situation is, it will change.
32. Don't take yourself so seriously. No one else does.

33. Believe in miracles.
34. God loves you because of who God is, not because of anything you did or didn't do.
35. Don't audit life. Show up and make the most of it now.
36. Growing old beats the alternative—dying young.
37. Your children get only one childhood.
38. All that truly matters in the end is that you loved.
39. Get outside every day. Miracles are waiting everywhere.
40. If we all threw our problems in a pile and saw everyone else's, we'd grab ours back.
41. Envy is a waste of time. Accept what you already have not what you need.
42. The best is yet to come...
43. No matter how you feel, get up, dress up, and show up.
44. Yield.
45. Life isn't tied with a bow, but it's still a gift."

Key Takeaways:

1. Read.
2. Smile.
3. Find a the bits of truth in there that apply to you and keep them in mind.

21. Preview Your Deathbed

If you knew your time had come, what would be your biggest regrets?

It's an intriguing question to consider, since it tells us what we might want to fix before we get there.

In a great book written by the Australian palliative nurse Bronnie Ware, she summarizes the top five regrets people had on their deathbeds.

Here is the list from Bronnie's blog ([bit.ly/mb-1210a](bit.ly/mb-1210a)):

1. I wish I'd had the courage to live a life true to myself, not the life others expected of me.

"This was the most common regret of all. When people realize that their life is almost over and look back clearly on it, it is easy to see how many dreams have gone unfulfilled. Most people had not honored even half of their dreams and had to die knowing that it was due to choices they had made, or not made.

It is very important to try and honor at least some of your dreams along the way. From the moment that you lose your health, it is too late. Health brings a freedom very few realize, until they no longer have it.

2. I wish I hadn't worked so hard.

"This came from every male patient that I nursed. They missed their children's youth and their partner's companionship. Women also spoke of this regret. But as most were from an older generation, many of the female patients had not been breadwinners. All of the men I nursed deeply regretted spending so much of their lives on the treadmill of a work existence.

By simplifying your lifestyle and making conscious choices along the way, it is possible to not need the income that you think you do. And by creating more space in your life, you become happier and more open to new opportunities, ones more suited to your new lifestyle.

3. I wish I'd had the courage to express my feelings.

"Many people suppressed their feelings in order to keep peace with others. As a result, they settled for a mediocre existence and never became who they were truly capable of becoming. Many developed illnesses relating to the bitterness and resentment they carried as a result.

We cannot control the reactions of others. However, although people may initially react when you change the way you are by speaking honestly, in the end it raises the relationship to a whole new and healthier level. Either that or it releases the unhealthy relationship from your life. Either way, you win.

4. I wish I had stayed in touch with my friends.

"Often they would not truly realize the full benefits of old friends until their dying weeks and it was not always possible to track them down. Many had become so caught up in their own lives that they had let golden friendships slip by over the years. There were many deep regrets about not giving friendships the time and effort that they deserved. Everyone misses their friends when they are dying.

It is common for anyone in a busy lifestyle to let friendships slip. But when you are faced with your approaching death, the physical details of life fall away. People do want to get their financial affairs in order if possible. But it is not money or status that holds the true importance for them. They want to get things in order more for the benefit of those they love. Usually though, they are too ill and weary to ever manage this task. It is all comes down to love and relationships in the end. That is all that remains in the final weeks, love and relationships.

5. I wish that I had let myself be happier.

"This is a surprisingly common one. Many did not realize until the end that happiness is a choice. They had stayed stuck in old patterns and habits. The so-called "comfort" of familiarity overflowed into their emotions, as well as their physical lives. Fear of change had them pretending to others, and to their selves, that they were content. When deep within, they longed to laugh properly and have silliness in their life again.

When you are on your deathbed, what others think of you is a long way from your mind. How wonderful to be able to let go and smile again, long before you are dying."

If you are interested in Bronnie's book, it can be found here:

bit.ly/mb-1210b

Key Takeaways:

1. Think about what you would regret the most if you found out suddenly that you were dying.

2. What are the barriers that stop you from achieving or fixings those items while you still can?

3. Be courageous: remove those barriers and prevent those regrets while there is still time.

22. Beyond Religion

Ethics for a Whole World

When to Read It

 If you liked the chapter about values, ethics, faith, and religion (see page 52), this book might be of interest to you. When asked "Which is the right religion?" His Holiness the Dalai Lama once replied: "Yours!" Beyond Religion promotes universally true values no matter what church you belong to. Not only an enjoyable read, it serves as great food for thought during the times you set aside for yourself.

What I liked About It

"A book that brings people together on the firm grounds of shared values, reminding us why the Dalai Lama is still one of the most important religious figures in the world." —Huffington Post, "Best Religious Books of 2011"

Ten years ago, in the best-selling "Ethics for a New Millennium," His Holiness the Dalai Lama proposed an approach to ethics based on universal rather than religious principles. With "Beyond Religion," he continues this dialogue at his most outspoken, elaborating and expounding on his vision in a secular way and showing the path to an ethical, happy, and spiritual life. Transcending the religion wars, he outlines a system of ethics for our shared world, one that makes a stirring appeal for a deep appreciation of our common humanity, offering us all a road map for improving human life on individual, community, and global levels.

"Cogent and fresh . . . This ethical vision is needed as we face the global challenges of technological progress, peace, environmental destruction, greed, science, and educating future generations." —Spirituality & Practice

The details

"Beyond Religion: Ethics for a Whole World" by H.H. Dalai Lama (Author), Alexander Norman (Contributor).

Amazon link

bit.ly/mb-1211

Three things to get out of this book:

1. A great answer to the question of which religion is right: yours!

2. A guide to your quest for happiness.

3. An interesting view on ethics in our shared world.

23. Guide to the Bodhisattva's Way of Life

A Buddhist Poem for Today

When to Read It

 This book is for those seeking a deeper delve into their value systems. It is one of the fundamental works of Buddhist teachings and a frequent subject of his Holiness the Dalai Lama's public teachings. While an interest in Buddhism will help you appreciate the thoughts presented in this book on a deeper level, one need not be a Buddhist to benefit from it. If you liked our chapter on meditation (see page 32), you will find this book a good starting point for your meditation sessions.

What I Liked About It

This famous and universally loved poem has inspired many generations of Buddhists and non-Buddhists since it was first composed in the eighth century by the famous Indian Buddhist master Shantideva.

This new translation, made possible under the guidance of Geshe Kelsang Gyatso, conveys the poetic beauty of the original, while preserving its full impact and spiritual insight.

Reading these verses slowly while contemplating their meaning has a profoundly liberating effect on the mind. The poem invokes special positive states of mind, moving from suffering and conflict to happiness and peace, and gradually introduces us to the entire Mahayana Buddhist path to enlightenment.

The Details

"Guide to the Bodhisattva's Way of Life: A Buddhist Poem for Today" By Shantideva (Author), Geshe Kelsang Gyatso (Translator), Neil Elliott (Translator).

Amazon link

bit.ly/mb-1212

Three things to get out of this book:

1. Interesting, lasting insights into Buddhist teachings.
2. A rich source of thoughts for calm contemplation.
3. A useful glossary to help navigate through this work of poetry.

24. De-Clutter Your Lifestyle

 If your financial options are limited and you just don't seem to make enough money, it might be a good time to review your costly habits.  A quick review will reveal some habits you're most likely aware of and expose others that might come as a surprise once you sum up exactly how much you spend on them.

Later in this book, I will speak about how de-cluttering your home can make a house that seemed too small feel right and spacious again (see page 105). The same principle applies to your financial life. De-cluttering your costly habits will free up income and give you financial room to breathe.

There are plenty of areas to de-clutter, but here are my top six recommendations.

Cars

There are cars that function to take us from point A to point B and then there are cars that must do much more than that. They have to impress the neighbors, to make a noise that feels powerful, they have to be fun to drive, and they have to give us the flexibility to do things we might never have to do, such as drive through three feet of river mud.

If you spend a lot of money on cars, consider changing your view of them from status symbols and toys back to transportation devices. Everything beyond the functions that transport you reliably and comfortably from two points are major money suckers you can easily avoid.

Home Entertainment and Gadgets

Sometimes it seems as if the size of a plasma TV is adversely correlated to the income of the owner. Don't fall into that trap. There will always be a higher resolution source of media, a larger TV, a better sound system, a more recent electronic gadget, and a more encompassing bundle of TV channels. Consider the role media should play in your life and determine a good level of media equipment that will provide that for you. Also remember that something you buy on credit is something you cannot afford.

Cigarettes

Enough said! Calculate how much you spend on cigarettes and there you go! We won't even mention the health benefits of becoming a non-smoker.

Going Out

An active social life is very important for your overall Life Balance, but obviously there are more expensive and more economical ways to socialize. Keep a log during an average month to find out how much you spend on going out. Once you can see where your money goes, see if you can reduce your spending by blending in a few less expensive restaurants, a few more home-cooked dinners, and a few more quality events with your friends or partner, like working out together, going on a hike, organizing a picnic, etc.

Travel

In general, people in the US and Japan have fewer vacation days available to them than Europeans. Their travel tends to be more domestic than international and they tend to spend more per day during those days of travel.

A recent study—the 2012 Morpace Omnibus report (bit.ly/mb-1301)–revealed that 45% of Americans rely on their credit cards or loans to pay for their vacation. Avoid falling into the trap of overspending for a trip you cannot actually afford.

Expensive Hobbies

Refurbishing vintage cars, keeping tropical fish, collecting rare comic books–the list of expensive hobbies is endless. While it is very important for your Life Balance to have time for yourself and to find things to do with your friends, think about how much you spend on your current hobby and see if you can shift that to an activity equally satisfying with less of the accompanying cost.

Conclusion

Consider de-cluttering your lifestyle. Examine your life goals and see if they tend more towards "being rich" or more towards "being happy." You might find that simplifying your hobbies will also simplify your life when you'll need less space in general to house your expensive stuff.

This is not about having less fun– on the contrary! Giving yourself more financial flexibility and less things to worry about will improve your Life Balance as well. So don't stop travelling. Don't stop having a hobby. Don't stop going out. Just see if you can find more economic ways of having the same amount of fun.

Key Takeaways:

1. See which of the above items you spend money on and calculate how much.

2. If you determine you do need to reduce your spending, try to cut out some bad habits or change them into more economical ones.

3. De-clutter your lifestyle to find simpler ways to have more fun.

25. When in Debt, Change Your Life

 The old adage "only spend what you have" doesn't seem to fit today's world anymore. Consumer debt is growing rapidly in Western countries and if you are in debt, it makes sense to examine the good and bad kinds of debt and see how you can change your life.

Bad Debt

Lifestyles differ not just around the world, but within countries, and even amongst friends and colleagues. No matter how well off we may be, there is always something more to strive or wish for: The bigger flat screen TV, the cooler car, the more exotic vacation.

Funding a lifestyle upgrade through debt is never a good idea. While credit cards are tempting temporary solutions to get the things you can't really afford, lifestyle purchases on borrowed money will get you into trouble.

The reason is simple. Your disposable income is your net salary minus your recurring payments and if your disposable income does not allow you to save money for future purchases, making these purchases today and postponing payment with money that won't come in the future is a bad idea. Matching your lifestyle to your income sounds obvious, but it's advice that definitely deserves a mention.

Times of Low Income

What if you lose your job? In temporary times of low income, it may be prudent to build a plan with a predefined grace period that can keep your spending levels almost at normal. This grace period is a short time of several weeks in which you will ideally find a position with a similar or higher income.

If, against all odds, you can't find a new job during your predefined grace period, you will need to reduce your spending as your unemployment continues.

While your lifestyle doesn't have to change immediately after you lose your job, you need to remain flexible and downgrade your spending until you have found a new position.

Is There Good Debt?

Borrowing money need not always be negative. Buying a home, replacing a critical item, and investing money are all examples of positive debt.

Buying a Home

Becoming a homeowner is an important step in many peoples' lives. In planning this step one doesn't consider only the monthly or annual income, but the expected income over a lifetime. A realistic estimation of how your income will evolve over time will show you the financial potential in purchasing a home. In many cases it will make perfect economic sense to borrow money from the bank and purchase a home rather than continue to pay rent every month.

Replacing a Critical Item

We all have critical items in our lives that need to remain functional. These may be items such as our cars or certain major household appliances. Depending on where you live and whether or not you have dependents, a broken down car or a broken washer and drier may have to be replaced immediately. While our definition of "critical" items may differ, a new TV, a new game console, or an expensive vacation should not be considered critical.

For real critical items, it makes sense to go into debt. However, make sure to build a tight short-term plan to repay the loan, so that the lifetime of the item you purchase is longer than that of your loan.

Investing Money

Another rare example of good debt is a specific area of investment.

With a no-risk investment that yields a higher return than what you are paying for the loan, borrowing money is a no-brainer. However, no-risk really should mean no-risk.

Another special case of positive debt is if you need to make a purchase but your saved money is invested and the investment comes with high termination fees. In this case it would be cheaper to borrow money for a few weeks or months, rather than pull your money out of your bank or investment.

Key Takeaways:

1. Do not fund a lifestyle upgrade through debt.

2. If you ever lose your job, have a tight plan with a grace period and an agreed savings plan mapped out until you find a new job.

3. Get financial advice on positive reasons to go in debt, including buying a home and balancing an investment.

26. Review Your Recurring Spending

 If you look at your checking account you will find that over the year, a significant amount of your expenditures are recurring items. Insurance policies, bank fees, media subscriptions, Internet, home, and cell phone packages are all examples where the wrong contract can cost you not only once, but continuously.

Fortunately, the Internet offers multiple comparison platforms for you to cut a better deal. Your friends may also be happy to offer advice as to which services they've recently found, are happy with, or are dissatisfied with.

Insurance

Start by making a list of which insurances you need. You may currently have too many or too few. Consider which insurances are required by law, e.g. car insurance or health insurance in certain countries. Even in these categories you will generally have a choice and you should compare plans carefully. Personal liability insurance and home insurance also come under this category.

Consider also insurance that may not be mandatory but may increase your peace of mind. Examples include insurance against broken glass in your home, the cost of legal advice in case of conflict, theft insurance for your bicycle, you name it. While these are losses you may potentially cover yourself, you may enjoy knowing that you are insured against these potentially costly risks.

I recommend creating an inventory of all the insurances you currently have. Create a simple table listing the category of each policy, its contract number, the company's contact details, the expiration and renewal date for the contract, and a short description of anything covered. Keep this inventory file handy and ideally save a copy in the cloud so that you may have it ready even if something happens to your home or if you need access to these details on the road. Depending on your termination clause for each policy, review your current contract regularly and switch if you find a better or more affordable offer. Eventually, you may be able to find cheaper deals for several, if not all of your policies.

Banking

Take a look at your banking expenses. These are account fees, credit card fees, transaction fees, and interest paid on credit card debt or loans. Summing up all these expenses may expose a significant yearly expenditure. Review to determine if you really need all those credit cards, if you can find a cheaper checking account, or if it makes sense to refinance money borrowed from the bank.

Phone, Web, and Media

Home and cell phone service, Internet service, and media consumption such as cable TV can represent a significant expenditure in your annual budget. You can save money by reviewing if you really need what you have subscribed to, or if you can reduce cost by consolidating several needs in a bundle, for example bundles that combine phone, Internet and cable TV. Reviewing your phone and Internet subscriptions may lead to some interesting insights and comparing these to current offers on the market could most likely get you a better deal with better service at lower cost.

Key Takeaways:

1. Create an insurance inventory and keep it in the cloud, e.g. on Dropbox.

2. List your expenditures for insurance policies, banking, and phone/internet/media to find out how much you spend in these categories.

3. Be aware of your termination deadlines and compare current market offers to what you currently have.

27. Self-employed and Successful

Know Your Strengths and Weaknesses

 If you're self-employed, you've probably created a business on particular talents or strengths you possess.

Technical experts will usually have turned a talent or aptitude into a profession and started their own business around it. This could be a great photographer or a skillful carpenter, a wonderful composer or a skilled doctor.

On the other hand, those with a talent for business are usually great at creating efficient processes, convincing others of their products and services, as well as asking the right price for the service and keeping on top of invoices.

Unfortunately, technical expertise and business talent might not always go hand in hand.

If you run your own business, you might know this feeling well. The quality of your work is superb. Your work is efficient. Yet, you may find it difficult to ask for more money, keep on top of paperwork and get those invoices sent out on time. You might wonder why your customers don't give you more business, pay you on time, and question if they are aware of your fullest capacities.

If some or all of the above is true, you have three options.

1. Learn the Missing Talent

Learning business acumen can be difficult for a technical expert and you may end up spending valuable time better invested in producing the product you are so good at. You may also find learning business to fall out of your comfort zone, yet if the thought has some appeal and you possess the free time, this first option might be right for you.

2. Find a Business Partner

You have been your own boss for a while and you like to follow your own rules. However, if your business is suffering from the symptoms above, consider finding a business partner. Bringing that business talent into your team and having somebody help you deal with customers, request the right prices, and organize processes in your business could be a key ingredient to your success as an entrepreneur. Finding a business partner if you are a technical expert is not easy, but the right partner could increase your success immensely.

3. Get a job

If learning the business trade is not for you and finding a business partner is not feasible, you might want to consider going back into employment. Finding a firm that allows you to shine in your technical field of expertise might provide you with the organizational framework to be really successful without the hassle of organizing your own business. Don't reject this option too early, but consider it carefully: If bad business skills are causing you to struggle, going back to employment could improve your life and bank balance significantly.

Key Takeaways:

1. If you are your own boss, but lack the business acumen to balance your technical talent, either seek to learn the business aspects you lack or...

2. ... find yourself a business partner or...

3. ... get a job as an employee to let your talent shine without the stress of running your own shop.

28. Are You Relatively Poor?

 How much money do you need to make to be rich? Or how little to be poor? Why is it that someone with your income might be considered rich amongst his friends and somebody with the same income, but in another situation, might consider himself poor?

Of course, every country and government will try to define thresholds to define rich and poor, and such definitions also depend strongly on your immediate environment.

If you are unhappy with your current financial situation, it might also be a question of perspective. Does it seem like your friends drive bigger cars, go on more exotic trips, and enroll their children in more exclusive private schools? Beware of comparing yourself with exorbitant friends or acquaintances—you have no way of knowing how they really pay for their lifestyles or if their material possessions truly make them happy (see the chapter on de-cluttering your lifestyle on page 83).

To live a happy and balanced life, measure yourself by your own standards. How much material wealth do you need to be content? What are you willing to give up for a higher material lifestyle?

Once you answer these questions, it should be easy to stop comparing yourself with seemingly more affluent people around you. If however, you find a change of perspective difficult or impossible to achieve, consider surrounding yourself with different people. If your rich buddies bring you down and fill you with negative feelings of greed and envy, try recalibrating your social environment with folks more in tune with your lifestyle.

Sometimes, feeling rich or feeling poor is merely a matter of changing your perspective—or changing the people you spend your time with.

Key Takeaways:

1. Ask yourself if your wealthier friends' lifestyle brings you down or creates feelings of envy.

2. If it does, change your perspective as to what you really need financially to be happy.

3. If that doesn't work, consider surrounding yourself with friends more in tune with your lifestyle.

29. Don't Fly Blind Financially

Is there too much month left at the end of your money? Do you just want to have a better idea of where your money goes? Having some structure in place for your finances, however minimal, allows you to be in control and identify problems early.

The lower your income, the better your planning needs to be. When it comes to finances, flying blind can be very dangerous. High debt on your credit cards, frequent surprises by unusual spending, or spending an unexpected influx of income on impulse purchases are all calls to improve your financial planning. Starting is easy...

You should consider the following three tools for planning your finances:

- A monthly household expense tracker.
- An annual finance plan.
- A life savings plan.

Household Expense Tracker

This tool is useful if you struggle to make it through a full month with your available funds. Start using an expense tracker to note how much money you spend in various categories. There are plenty of tools available on the web or even as an app for your smart phone. Pick the one you like best and use it to see where your money goes. Track two or three months and you'll be able to identify areas where you can save without impacting your life quality too much.

Once you can more comfortably make it through a month with your available income, consider eliminating the household expense tracker altogether. Its main benefit is to identify problem areas and once you understand your spending behavior, the ongoing effort might not be a wise investment of your time.

The Annual Finance Plan

Planning finances ahead for a full year makes sense for everyone, no matter what their income. Writing down your expected income on one side of a piece of paper and your anticipated spending on the other side will give you a good idea of your financial flexibility.

Make sure to include all sources of income on the income side, including your salary, potential income from your investments, and any other sources. Remember to deduct your anticipated taxes, so that you're looking at only your available income.

On the expenses side, categorize your spending into recurring spending (for example ongoing household expenses, car, insurances, rent or mortgage), special items during the year (for example holiday presents or vacations) as well as money you plan to save.

Try to separate your planned savings into three categories:

1. A reserve for unforeseen events, such as a major appliance failure or a car break-down.

2. Savings for larger purchases, such as a new car, a particular gadget you want to treat yourself to, or a renovation to your home.

3. Last but not least, consider reserving some money towards your retirement. This is especially important if you are self-employed or a freelancer.

Life Savings Plan

A life savings plan can help you forecast the amount of savings you can afford to put aside for after you stop working. Since there are many different ways of investing your savings and many different tax rules and subsidies that differ by country, it might help to secure the help of a professional financial planner when building your life savings plan.

As with all plans, you will find that the tools above only provide a framework. Life does tend to surprise us every day. However, the benefit of having such tools in place is that you can now compare your plan with reality and start to draw consequences from what you see.

A good starting point to look for financial planning tools on the web is www.nomoredebts.org

Key Takeaways:

1. Use a household expense tracker if you have trouble making it through the month with your available income.

2. Make sure to have an annual finance plan to determine your financial flexibility.

3. Use the life savings plan to get ready for your retirement— with or without the help of a financial planner.

30. Do You Have the Right Home?

 Granted, this is a strange question, but if you wouldn't reside where you live today and started from scratch drawing a list of requirements, what would you write down? Do you like representative or cozy, centrally located or quiet, green and lush or practical? Does your home need to be close to the office or close to the airport? Do you need a guest room for all of your friends who come and visit or an office to work from—or both?

Now, when you compare your list with the attributes of your home, how do you score? Be very honest in evaluating the characteristics of your home and decide if it meets your requirements and ads to your balance in life. If it doesn't and there is no easy fix, consider moving - do not settle for something that eats your energy on an ongoing basis.

Key Takeaways:

1. Create a clean sheet of paper list of what you need from your home.
2. Compare how your current home scores against this list.
3. Fix the gaps where possible.
4. If all that doesn't help, consider moving.

31. My Home is My (Affordable) Castle

The Financial Burden

 Whether your home is just a place to sleep at night or the sanctuary in which you recharge your batteries and meet with friends and family, it plays an elemental role in maintaining your Life Balance.

Renting, financing or owning your home will most likely be a significant item in your annual budget. This includes rent or mortgage payments, utility bills, tax, repair and maintenance, and many other spending items related to your home.

If you feel that the combined cost for living in your home does not stress your budget, then congratulations, you are done with this chapter!

However, if you feel that you spend too much on your home—or don't make enough to afford it—then here are a few thoughts for you to consider:

- Determine how much you spend on an annual basis for your home. Include all relevant costs such as rent or mortgage payments, utility bills, property taxes, repair and maintenance. If you pay for cleaning services, yard maintenance, or other such services, include the cost of them as well.

- Calculate the percentage of your annual available income that you spend on your home.

- Now perform an honest evaluation of your findings. Does the result feel right? Or do you think that you are spending more than what you can afford on your home? If the latter is the case, then chances are your home will de-energize you rather than recharge your batteries. It will take away from your Life Balance rather than enhance it.

If what you spend on home costs is out of proportion, then here are your three simple options:

Reduce the Cost

Easier said than done sometimes. Let's build a list of ideas for you to consider:

Rent

- Has your rental agreement been in place for some time? If the level of rent paid in your area has changed over time, then there may be a chance to negotiate a lower rent with your landlord.

- Do you pay for services around your home that you could perform yourself? If you were willing to do the mowing yourself, for example, then you could cut that cost from your list and perhaps even reduce your rent if you perform this task for other units as well.

Mortgage

- If you own your home and have financed part of it with a mortgage, then maybe the interest level has changed since you signed your deal. Mortgage refinancing is such a broad and complex field that I will not go into detail here, but if you have a mortgage that is several years old and have never considered refinancing it, then you may want to look into it. The only bit of advice I will give here is to use a well-known and trustworthy service for refinancing, for example your own bank or a similar one.

Utility Bills

- If you live in a country with a deregulated utility market, then you will be able to choose from several companies providing gas, electricity or water to your home. If that is the case and you are still buying from what used to be the monopoly or government owned provider, chances are you are paying too much. Review the current pricing for utilities in your market and see how much you could save if you change your provider. If you live in a market with a single utilities provider, follow their recommendations on how to improve efficiency and make small changes that can result in lower overall costs.

- Another important cost factor is how your home is connected to the outside world. Telephony, internet connectivity, and entertainment like cable TV can add significant cost to your annual budget. Be aware of what you really need and compare offers in your region. Changing providers may either save you some real cash or get you more for the same.

Repair and Maintenance

- The first general bit of advice here is to not put off required maintenance to save money. The resulting damages may far exceed what you can save.

- The second recommendation is to transfer a regular monthly amount of money into a savings or similar type of account to save specifically for repair and maintenance that only occurs yearly. This way you spread the burden more evenly throughout the year to help deal with the cost once it hits you.

Make more money

This is also easier said than done, but if your spend on home-related costs is too high and you can't reduce it further, then finding a better paying job is one way of dealing with the challenge. Be sure not to fix one problem by creating another one—if your current job is what you love doing, if the commute is not too far, and if changing jobs involves a lot of risk, then think twice.

Move

If you can't reduce your home-related cost and also can't get a better paying job, then you should consider moving into a more affordable home. Play with that thought for a while and see how it feels. If your current home adds so much to your quality of life and its balance, then you will feel it and the thought of moving will feel wrong.

However, if it is only the effort of moving that scares you, but lower costs and a smaller place to maintain sound tempting in general, then mull it over and go house hunting.

Key Takeaways:

1. Determine how much you spend on an annual basis for your home.

2. If your spend on home cost is out of proportion, then reduce the cost, make more money, or move!

32. De-Clutter Your Life

 Before you de-clutter your life, let's start with your home! If you feel that you lack space at home, that certain parts of your home cannot be used for their designated purpose because of the clutter there or that your home quickly falls into chaos, then consider a few of the following:

Untidy Areas

Every home needs untidy areas—define where they should be. You constantly bring things home that do not immediately disappear: luggage from your last trip, parcels from the UPS guy, that clunky thing you bought at the garage sale. Grant yourself some space that is a designated chaos zone and develop a discipline to limit the chaos to these places.

Allowing for well-defined untidy areas in your home will make it much easier to keep the rest of your home nice and cozy.

Don't Grow into Your Home

Remember when you moved in? That great feeling of space and closets that had a system to them? If those times are long gone then you have grown into your home like a plant grows into its pot until it becomes too small. In my family we always loved our rule of "If you bring something into the house, something equally large has to go!" Of course there are exceptions to that rule (my baby daughter for example!), but if a family member buys a pair of shoes, one pair will go. A new TV, the old one goes. Ten new books, some of the vacation paperbacks that nobody will ever read again will go.

In and out don't always happen at the same time, but try to make a point of cleaning out clutter on a regular basis. Sell or donate and recycle, or dispose of. Ebay and Amazon are great places to sell things that still have value. Charities usually have a use for many things that otherwise would have to be thrown away: clothing, furniture, even old cars.

Hold On to Memories

Make sure to avoid one pitfall of spring cleaning: Don't let go of memories too quickly. If it comes with a fond memory, then the in-and-out rule need not automatically apply!

Key Takeaways:

1. Define untidy areas in your home.
2. Don't grow into your home—have an in-and-out rule.
3. Hold on to memories.

33. Is Your Home a Chore or Hobby?

 Keeping your garden pretty can be a wonderful way to relax after work and keeping a cozy old house in shape is a fulfilling hobby if you are a skilled handyman. But if you don't like gardening or if you don't have the time to spend on your house, a garden or an old house can quickly turn into a stressful burden. If that is the case for you, consider the following:

Hire Some Help

See if you can afford someone to help with the garden or the house. It might be quite an investment, but the time you buy can pay off well if you can recharge and perform better at work.

Get Some Gadgets

Gadgets can be wonderful time savers too. One of my personal favorite time savers around the house is my automated lawn mower (see page 111); it works silently and throughout the week so that I no longer have to spend hours on the weekend mowing the lawn.

Stay Realistic

If you buy an old house and want to turn it into a modern mansion with the latest and greatest features, be prepared to spend an inordinate amount of time and money. Make sure you have a clear understanding of the limits of your home, your skills, your funds and the time you have available.

If maintaining your home continues to be a burden, as a last resort, consider finding a new home and moving to a place that will make a positive change in your Life Balance.

Key Takeaways:

1. See if you can afford help for your garden or your house.
2. Check out some of the time-saving gadgets available.
3. Be realistic when setting your home goals.
4. As a last resort, consider moving.

34. Commuting to Work

How much time do you spend commuting to work every day? If you said 25 minutes, that's the national average in the US, and that leaves a 50% chance that you spend more time than that. At 25 minutes a day (back and forth together), you spend 100 hours a year or about half a year during your life commuting to work. If it is more like 50-60 minutes a day, just double this to get a feeling for how much time you spend to bridge the distance between your home and your work.

You know the saying "Love it, change it, or leave it!" Let's see how that can work for you here.

A Good Use of Time

Make the best of your commute by doing things during the commute you would otherwise do at other hours of the day. Check-in with co-workers, friends or family members who are in a good position to take your call at that time of the day. Mentally engage and disengage with work on your way from and to home so that your partner or family has your full attention while you are at home. Change your car for a bike to combine commuting with your workout.

Spend Less Time

See how you can affect your commute by reducing the time you spend on it. Might your job allow you to change your hours to avoid traffic? Might you work from home for part of the day or a part of the week?

New Job or Home?

If you can't love it and you can't change it, then maybe you have to leave it. What would it take to either change jobs or move somewhere else to reduce your commute? What seems to be a small saving of time per day can easily sum up to a significant amount of time over the years, so consider how this additional time could help improve your Life Balance.

Key Takeaways:

1. Make the best of your commute.
2. Reduce the time spent on your commute.
3. If all that doesn't help, consider changing your job or moving.

35. Get a Robot to Help in Your Garden

🔧 If you have a house with a garden, chances are you have to spend several hours a week maintaining that garden—and mowing the lawn probably takes up a big chunk of that time.

Getting a robotic lawnmower to help you with that task is a wise investment. Not only does it free up your time for other tasks, it might also take a frequent source of conflict out of your family life and allows your lawn to look perfect every day.

Here are the five things I love about robotic lawnmowers:

1. They have become fairly sophisticated and affordable. While early models were much more expensive and leaving much to be desired on the technological side, today there are several reliable brands to choose from that deliver consistently good results.

2. They are easy to set up. Most of the systems use a perimeter wire around the area that needs to be mowed and once the wire is laid out and the charging station is set up, you pick the days per week and the hours per day when you want your new gardener to work for you. Depending on the size of your lawn, your robotic mower might work three to seven days for two to four hours per day.

3. They are silent and fun to watch. During its assigned working hours your robotic lawnmower will go back and forth within the perimeter wire to mow your lawn. It will start in one direction and make a random turn once it reaches the perimeter and then repeat this process until the working hours are over. Since your robotic lawnmower

uses silently rotating cutter-like blades, it hardly makes any noise and can even operate during the night.

4. They are incredibly convenient. Not only do they save you time on mowing, they also save the effort of collecting and disposing of the cut grass. Since the mower works almost every day, such small bits of grass can remain on the lawn and even serve as fertilizer.

5. It's a really smart solution. Your lawn will look fresh-cut every day and your robotic gardener doesn't mind slopes or obstacles in your garden or even the complex shapes of your property. Your perimeter wire allows you to create an easy-to-navigate environment for your robotic lawnmower.

The robotic lawnmower is definitely one of my favorite time savers!

Amazon Link

bit.ly/mb-1406

Key Takeaways:

1. Think about how much time per week you spend on mowing your lawn.
2. Consider a robotic lawnmower to free up this time.
3. Enjoy the additional benefits of a consistently clean lawn, silent mowing, and not having to clean up and dispose of cut grass.

36. A Space Age Vacuum Cleaner

Before I tested this little sucker, I had almost given up hope on handheld vacuum cleaners. Now we managed to find one that will help you clean your home and many other places without having to pull the giant vacuum out of the closet every time.

How It Improves Your Life Balance

In our test, the Dyson quickly became one of the most used household utensils of the day. Small but powerful, it makes cleaning up breadcrumbs, cobwebs, dust, and the like, well ….fun. And it's super portable making it quite the timesaver.

More Cool Things

- Its suction is digital, which means it has six minutes to deliver you constant power.
  After that, it doesn't fade out, but stops until recharged.

- It's very easy to clean: just hold it over your trashcan, press a button and the floor of the tank opens and empties itself. No big messy vacuum bags to wrestle with.

- It's great to clean your car too.

Amazon Link

bit.ly/mb-1407

Three things to use it for:

1. A room by room dusting spree.
2. A mediator for a spontaneous after breakfast breadcrumb fight.
3. A quick tidy up of your car.

37. When Being Healthy Is Not Achievable

 While many people are getting excited about health, fitness, working out and getting in shape, some may be dealing with health conditions that have a severe impact on their day to day. Birth defects, diseases, severe or terminal illnesses or other forms of physical challenges have the power to put our entire lives into another context.

Whether it's the inability to do what others do, the pain we have to endure or the expectation that life might end sooner than we had hoped it would–these issues are a burden that can, but don't necessarily have to throw our lives off balance.

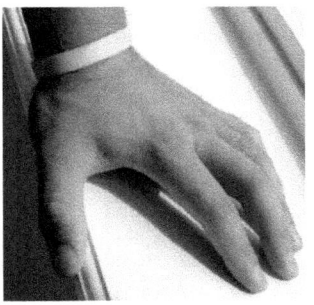

Why do some deal better with health challenges than others? Why can we meet terminally ill cancer patients who seem better balanced and happier than a friend with the flu?

This was one of the big mysteries in life for me until someone explained this as a very simple mathematical equation to me:

Suffering = Pain – Purpose

What does that mean? When I explained this to my 8-year-old daughter who has a genetic defect herself, I asked her: "Honey, when you get a flu shot, do you cry?"

"Of course not, Daddy!" was her reply.

My second question to her was: "But when someone at school pricks you with the same size needle–would you cry?"

"Yes, I guess I would," was her reply.

That's the explanation right there: The *pain* of being pricked with a needle is the same in the flu shot as well as in the school incident. But the flu shot offers the *purpose* of protection from an annoying or even dangerous infection; hence the *suffering* is small to non-existent.

It takes herculean efforts to translate this equation into a life situation with severe health issues, though the same principle is at work. For patients and family alike, finding a cause and a purpose helps deal with health challenges. The cancer patient who writes a book to tell his story for others to benefit from. The AIDS patient who volunteers in a charity for HIV prevention. The injured war veteran who fights for others who are affected even worse than himself. All of these are examples of how creating a purpose can balance the pain and reduce the suffering.

Key Takeaways:

1. Search your soul regarding the physical hardships in your life. What could be your purpose—small or big—to balance the pain in order to reduce the suffering?

2. If you have a health issue yourself or in your family, try balancing your pain with purpose. Find a cause to support or a change you can make to help YOU deal with it.

38. Sleep Well

 Get enough sleep! Is it that simple and true for everyone? This bit of advice is so obvious that it's almost not worth mentioning, except that it's so critical to your health that it must be mentioned. Sleep deprivation can wreak havoc on every aspect of your life, so get some sleep!

However, the need for sleep varies according to individuals and age. Ask yourself:

- Do you need a consistent amount of sleep? Can you handle draining your batteries during the week and recharging them when you sleep in on the weekend?

- How many hours of sleep are best for you? Too little will leave your weary, feeling uncomfortable and making you susceptible to infections or other health problems. Too much sleep—if there is such a thing—can cause health issues and make some of us feel guilty for wasting the day etc.

- What is the best sleep environment is for you? Do you need the room totally dark or not so dark? Are you ok with some noise or do you need total silence? Are you ok with the sleep environment you currently have (pillows, mattress etc.) or does it make you toss and turn?

We all need to allow for a certain amount of flexibility in our sleep schedules and environment, but practicing good sleep habits will help you get the right amount and the best quality of sleep for you.

You may need to invest in making your sleep environment just right for you—new pillows, curtains or blinds, or moving to a different room that is more quiet—but the rewards will be great.

For more information:

- Harvard Business Review Blog Network: Sleep is more important than food (bit.ly/mb-1502a)
- Health.harvard.edu: The importance of sleep: Six reasons not to scrimp on sleep (bit.ly/mb-1502b)
- Apa.org: Why sleep is important and what happens when you don't get enough (bit.ly/mb-1502c)
- Helpguide.org: How much sleep do you need? (bit.ly/mb-1502d)

Key Takeaways:

1. Determine your personal sleep requirements regarding sleep routine, amount, and environment.
2. Make the necessary changes to your sleep habits and environment.
3. Stay flexible, but make sure you meet your requirements most of the time.

39. Thoughts Before You Sleep

When we sleep, our brain has a tendency to rework and process the thoughts and worries we mulled on directly before falling asleep. Teachers are familiar with this phenomenon, which is why they may encourage students to study directly before sleeping. While this may be helpful for an upcoming test, concerns about your job, relationships or the future can create stress dreams or disturb the quality of your sleep and affect how you face an upcoming day. Instead of rehashing a problem that will carry on into the next morning, try motivating yourself with the following:

Two Positive Things

We're all familiar with lying in bed agonizing over the chores and work tasks, or even arguments we've had earlier in the day. "I have to finish this...", "If only I had said this to him!" but how often do we spend time lingering over the positives? Instead of thinking about what you have to do or could have done, find two positive things that have happened to you that day and spend the time before you sleep going over them.

They can be something momentous, like a large milestone achieved at work—but they can be as simple as a nice lunch you had with your colleague, finally catching up with the laundry, an internet funny, an episode of a show you enjoy. Hearing a piece of good news about someone in your family. A day of nice weather. Challenge yourself to find the pleasant portions of your past day and focus on those while you drift off to sleep. Your work and worries will still be waiting for you when you wake up, but your sleep will have been more restful and you will face your day in a more positive frame of mind.

Avoid the Negative

If you are a person who has trouble falling asleep due to worry about the day's events, it might help to make a cut-off point in the evening after which you won't watch news, or read news sites on the internet; respond to work related emails (or personal emails that are potentially embroiling). Use the last waking hours of your day to read, catch up with your partner, watch something amusing—take a walk. Give yourself positive things to consider before you go to sleep.

Key Takeaways:

1. Take a moment to find two positive things about your day and go over them in your mind before you go to sleep.

2. Make a cut-off point in the evening for reading emails and articles if you are a person who loses sleep thinking too much about upcoming tasks or negative news.

3. Remember that your problems will be there, whether you lose sleep over them or not. Leave daytime for solving problems and nighttime for sleeping.

40. Eat Well and Exercise

 Step away from the Nutella and get on your bike! It turns out that what you learned in school as a kid is actually true—eating right and exercising makes for a happier, and perhaps longer, life. So, work out, walk, ride your bike, take the stairs, park the car in the farthest reaches of the parking lot, whatever. Just do whatever works for you to get and stay fit.

If you need motivation, try this:

- Define your personal weight thresholds into zones: green, yellow and red zone

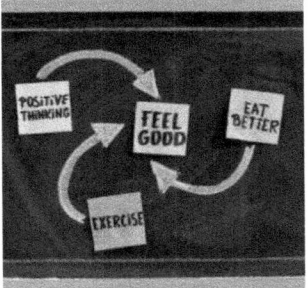

- Specify what you want to restrict yourself from when entering the yellow zone, for example:

    o No use of elevators, unless you have to carry heavy stuff or it's more than x floors up.

    o Only one glass of alcohol during social events.

    o No excuses for not working out.

    o Nothing but the main food item and veggies on your plate.

    o You get the idea—make up your own list!

- Finally, define more serious sanctions if you enter the red zone, for example:

    o No desserts.

    o No alcohol.

- Five workouts per week, even if it's just a walk or a few sit-ups in the morning.
- You get the idea—make up your own list.

These tips may help you to either maintain or achieve a healthy state of nutrition and body weight. Be patient and gentle though—better to set your thresholds for green, yellow, and red carefully and reduce them over time, than to be unrealistic and frustrate yourself with constant punishment in the red zone.

Key Takeaways:

1. Define your personal weight thresholds into zones: green, yellow, and red.

2. Specify what you want to restrict yourself from when entering the yellow or red zone.

3. Be realistic when setting your thresholds—better to reduce them over time than to frustrate and demotivate yourself by trying to cut out too much at one time.

41. Explore Alternative Medicine

 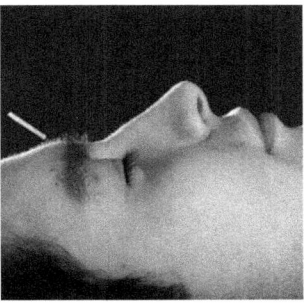 Explore alternative medicine not only as an adjunct to traditional medicine, but also as a preventative measure—chiropractic is great for the aches and pains that come with desk jobs, and who couldn't use a massage or quiet time to meditate or just be? Most insurance plans offer some benefits for alternative therapies, so take advantage of what they have to offer.

Key Takeaways:

1. Find out what type of alternative medicine benefits your health insurance offers.

2. Decide which methods you want to try to enhance your well-being.

3. Ask friends and relatives for recommendations based on their experiences with alternative treatments.

42. Stop Sitting

 Who knew that sitting could kill you dead? It's easy to fix though: just stop sitting. Recent studies show that too much sitting has a high negative impact on your body, so get up and move around throughout the day wherever you are.

Try to incorporate the following into your routine if your day includes much sitting:

- Complement your desk with a desk element that allows you to work standing up.
- Get a wireless headset for your desk phone that allows you to pace up and down while in phone conversations.
- Make a point of walking to your colleagues' desks for brief conversations rather than writing an email.
- On a nice day, leave the car behind and walk to that one place you were just about to drive to.

For more information

- NYTimes.Com: Is sitting a lethal activity? (bit.ly/mb-1505a)
- Sitting is killing you: (bit.ly/mb-1505b)

Key Takeaways:

1. Incorporate more standing into your daily routine to reduce sitting time.
2. Look for opportunities to walk instead of driving your car.

43. Don't Worry About Stress

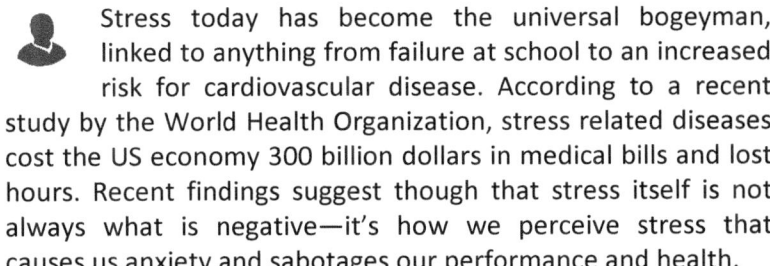

Stress today has become the universal bogeyman, linked to anything from failure at school to an increased risk for cardiovascular disease. According to a recent study by the World Health Organization, stress related diseases cost the US economy 300 billion dollars in medical bills and lost hours. Recent findings suggest though that stress itself is not always what is negative—it's how we perceive stress that causes us anxiety and sabotages our performance and health.

Is All Stress Bad?

Hans Selye was the first to write about General Adaption Syndrome (or stress syndrome) in 1936. He recognized that when the body is confronted with a demand, it goes under what we now call stress, by releasing certain hormones such as adrenaline and cortisol. At the time, Selye divided stress into two components: eustress (literally good stress) was the positive stress that fosters learning, growth and even victory. Distress was the negative stress that causes anxiety, depression, and has been linked to disease. Selye recognized that the body's response to both types of stresses was the same: increased heart rate, rapid breathing, and perspiration. Since then, the responses have been conflated into one category of impending negative stress, when in reality, these responses may just as well be construed as our bodies getting pumped up to meet a challenge.

From a Negative to a Positive Stress Response

In a recent study, subjects were shown videos that emphasized our bodies' stress responses (such as sweaty palms, increased heart rate and rapid breathing) as a positive sign of the body preparing to face a challenge. Later, when these subjects were deliberately put into stressful situations and their bodies predictably responded, they were able to stay much calmer than subjects who did not view a video on a positive stress response—or subjects who viewed a video that showed the response as a sign of anxiety and fear.

In another study, subjects who claimed to be concerned about their own stress levels were shown to have a much higher rate of stress related disease and death than subjects who objectively had similarly stressful jobs, but were not so consciously concerned about stress. This all goes to show that what may be stressing us out—is stressing about stress.

Reach Out to Relieve Stress

Psychologist Kelly McGonigal encourages people not only to view the stress response as a positive reaction of your body facing a challenge—but also to reach out. One hormone created by the pituitary gland during the stress response is oxytocin, also called the cuddle hormone, because it is the hormone that urges humans to seek contact with other humans. Oxytocin is released to protect the body from stress and the more we seek out situations that release it (such as situations where we help or have contact with others), the more the hormone strengthens the actual heart, creating what McGonigal calls 'the biology of courage.'

Obviously, tight deadlines, long hours and vigorous exams do create palpable, negative stress. However, by recognizing the body's responses as possibly positive instead of anxious reactions to stress, we can harness these responses to face the stressful task at hand, rather than view stress entirely as a harmful phenomenon.

For More Information

Go to bit.ly/mb-1506 to see Kelly McGonigal's video about how we perceive stress on YouTube:

Key Takeaways:

1. Remember that there is good stress and bad stress, but what is most negative for our health is how much we worry about stress.

2. The next time you find yourself in a stressful situation, think about your increased heart rate and butterflies as positive signs of being psyched up to meet the challenge rather than a precursor to failure.

3. Reach out more and release some healthy oxytocin. The more you reach out in environments of social stress to make contact with and help others, the more hormones your body releases and the more resilient you become to this type of stress.

44. Your Recharge Toolbox

Sixteen Great Ways to Re-Energize During the Day

It happens to your smart phone—the battery dies during the day and leaves you stranded without your favorite gadget, cut off from the world. But it also happens to you—your energy gets drained during the day and leaves you demotivated, uninspired or short-tempered.

Keep this list handy and pick your favorite recharging activity from it whenever your energy level drops. You'll see: your battery will get a boost and carry you through your day.

- **Be outside**
  Go for a walk or a run and enjoy the air, the sun and the weather.

- **Read something pleasant or inspiring**
  It helps sometimes to deal with something completely different.

- **Slow down and do one thing at a time**
  Observe how good you can be at things if you focus.

- **Exercise**
  Do your favorite exercise and enjoy the rush.

- **Take a nap**
  Even fifteen minutes will work.

- **Be silent and give your thoughts some room**
  Go for a walk, sit in a quiet place, take a bath, meditate.

- **Have a good conversation**
  Listen actively to someone you care about.

- **Change your point of view**
  Depolarize by trying to find three good arguments for their point of view.

- **Show compassion**
  You can't rescue everyone, but you can put yourself in their shoes and appreciate their struggle.

- **Imagine something new**
  Find a solution for something that bothers you.

- **Ask someone for help**
  You always help others; let them show their gratitude.

- **Fix a small nuisance**
  Because it feels great to finally change that light bulb.

- **Let go of something**
  Things in your closet, your bad habits, stuff you don't need.

- **Meet a new person**
  Hi, I have seen you a few times here and I wanted to introduce myself.

- **Perform an act of kindness**
  Help, compliment, make peace with, listen to, or invite someone.

- **Enjoy (!) a meal**
  Just good healthy food, you, and—maybe—a nice person to talk to.

What these activities have in common is that you will feel great and re-energized after any of them. They are the feel-good, do-good alternative to eating a bag of chips when you feel down and they work so much better.

Add your favorite recharging activities to this list and make a point of picking one every time you feel your energy drain away.

You can download a wall hanger format as well as a wallet format of this list (bit.ly/mb-1507) or refer to the resource section in the back of this book for a tear-out sheet of the two so that you can keep this list handy (see page 233).

Key Takeaways:

1. Note when your energy level drops during the day. Often this is not physical fatigue, but lack of positive energy in your day.

2. Test the activities from the list above to find out which of them work best for you to boost your energy.

3. Download and print the list to keep it handy and add your own favorite activities to it.

45. Burn Away Your Mosquito Bites

 Summer is the right time for the great outdoors. Friends and family can come together to enjoy barbecuing, camping, gardening—now if we could just eliminate the mosquito bites!

Luckily, there's a cool gadget available with surprising technology:

The Therapik is a temperature based anti-itch device based on a very simple, scientifically proven principle. Most insect venom is thermolabile, that is to say, sensitive to heat. If you apply heat in the specific temperature range necessary to neutralize the venom, you can provide instant relief from the pain and itch experienced from mosquito bites, bee stings, fire ants, jellyfish stings, and bites from up to 20,000 other species. This mosquito bite reliever is a handheld device that creates an endurable heat that, when applied to the affected area, relieves pain and itch from insect bites and stings.

How It Improves Your Life Balance

Go enjoy your summer again without the suffering from itchy bites.

More Cool Things

- These devices are really compact; perfect for beaching, camping, etc.
- Some devices have a setting for kids and less heat makes the application suitable for sensitive skin as well.

Amazon Link

bit.ly/mb-1508

Key Takeaways:

Use this gadget for itching bite relief.

46. Is Your Scale Online?

 If not, get yourself a scale that connects to the Wi-Fi in your home. The good ones come with an app for your mobile so you can check your progress on the go.

How It Improves Your Life Balance

If it's one of your health objectives to lose or maintain your weight, then you might need some motivation. Research proves that you are more successful in reducing or maintaining your body weight if you step on the scale every day, which is why we tested the Withings *Wifi Bodyscale* together with the corresponding app for iOS. Logging each weighing result and presenting it in a cool app makes it hard for you to ignore if the line points upwards. That makes a Wi-Fi scale with an app an ideal tool for conscious weight management.

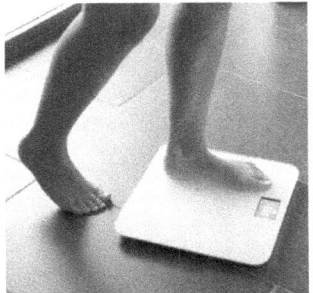

More Cool Things

- The scale can manage multiple family members and present the results in separate curves.

- In our test we defined two thresholds for our tester, which created a bad, medium and a good zone. Together with sanctions (for example no dessert in the bad zone, stairs instead of elevator in the medium zone, see page 121) this created a very effective system to manage weight.

Amazon Link

bit.ly/mb-1509

Use it to:

1. Create a playful incentive to step on the scale every day–it helps!

2. Manage several family members with one scale.

3. Define good, medium and bad zones, with corresponding rewards and sanctions.

Part 3 Life Balance Advice for Your Relationships

Your Partner—Your Friends—Your Family

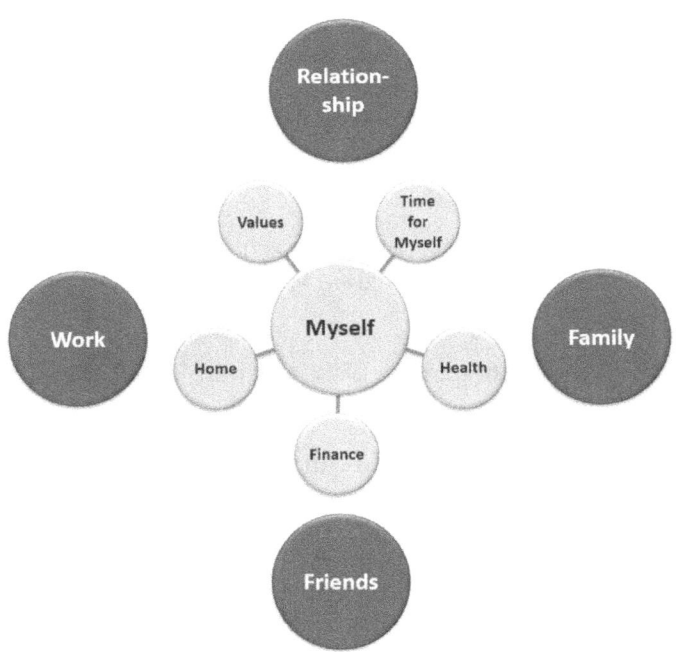

1. Alone Time With Your Partner

 Our constantly connected world makes it hard to focus on relationship imbalances, but if we pay some attention, we may find that we give too much time to our children, our work, and our chores—and that too little time remains for the partner who was once the most important person in our life.

The problem won't solve itself and while it may seem sadly unspontaneous, a plan gives you a starting point to ensure you don't neglect this important relationship.

Do yourself and your partner a favor and make it a priority to set aside some time each week to nurture your relationship:

- Plan for time where you are not a parent, but a spouse, i.e. plan to spend time with your partner without the kids.

- Plan to spend time with your partner without whatever device usually captures your attention.

- Do the things you once enjoyed together—or try something new. It could be a new sport or a language you learn together.

Whether once a week, every fortnight, or once a month, make sure you put it into your calendar and actually create a few special hours with a babysitter organized and your iPhone at home. Give your partner your full attention during this time, not as the parent of your children, the manager of your household or the partner in your business—but as your life-partner and friend.

Key Takeaways:

1. Get started by organizing a special activity like dinner, movies, a nice walk, a picnic etc. every week, fortnight or month.

2. Make sure the logistics all work, i.e. the babysitter is there, the table reserved, the tickets purchased.

3. Agree with your partner on how often you want to make this happen and then make it a part of your regular family calendar.

2. Trip of Love—Looking for Places to Go?

Whether you need time for yourself, want to take your partner on a trip, or are looking for a destination to explore with your friends, there are many worthwhile adventures out there. Different from the business travel we have to do, your personal journeys are pages in the diary of your life.

While this is a general reminder to include travel on your action list, I also want to give you some destinations to start with.

To Get You Started

The New York Times quite recently published a wonderful list of the 46 places to go to. This exotic list lets your imagination soar high and definitely gets your travel juices flowing:

1. **Rio de Janeiro –**
   Because the whole world will be there.

2. **Marseille France –**
   On the Mediterranean. Art and plenty of it.

3. **Nicaragua –**
   It's eco-! And the food is good! Enough said.

4. **Accra, Ghana –**
   A buzzing metropolis ready for business and pleasure.

5. **Bhutan –**
   A pristine Buddhist enclave opens, with care.

6. **Amsterdam, the Netherlands –**
   A decade later, museums reopen and are fancier than ever.

7. **Houston, Texas –**
   What's big in Texas? Culture and food.

8. **Rossland, British Columbia –**
    Fasten your skis. A quiet peak joins the big leagues.

9. **New Delhi, India –**
    Come for the new Metro, stay for where it takes you.

10. **Istanbul, Turkey –**
    Next Eurail stop: culture central.

11. **Singapore –**
    Green shoots in a financial capital.

12. **Montenegro –**
    A Balkan gem that is small, spectacular – and cheap.

13. **White Salmon River, Washington –**
    A river runs free for the first time in a century.

14. **Hvar, Croatia –**
    Explore the quieter side of a jet setters' haven.

15. **Mongolia –**
    The welcome mat is out for one million tourists.

16. **The Big Island, Hawaii –**
    Feasting on Hawaii's less visited isle.

17. **Philippines –**
    A surfing and beach destination goes deluxe.

18. **Vernazza, Italy –**
    After destruction, a Cinque Terre village blooms again.

19. **The Kimberley, Australia –**
    Adventure in the outer reaches of the Outback.

20. **Ningxia, China –**
    Chinese wine? Take a sip.

21. **The Adirondacks, N.Y. –**
    Backwoods New York is about to get more glam.

22. **Oslo, Norway** –
    A waterfront is stealing the Scandinavian spotlight.

23. **Constantia, South Africa** –
    A vineyard-heavy suburb gets a makeover.

24. **Lithuania** –
    An overlooked beer destination in the Baltics.

25. **Burgos, Spain** –
    An ancient city with a fresh face and culinary buzz.

26. **Lens, France** –
    Is the next Bilbao in northern France?

27. **Changbaishan China** –
    An Asian skiing spot gets supersized.

28. **Porto, Portugal** –
    Finally, places worthy of Porto's vintages – at table wine prices.

29. **Puerto Rico** –
    A spate of new hotels and restaurants animates the island.

30. **Koh Phangan, Thailand** –
    A party island goes upscale and family-friendly.

31. **Kalpitiya, Sri Lanka** –
    An Indian Ocean hideaway to visit before development descents.

32. **Jackson Hole, Wyoming** –
    Faster flights and lifts where the Buffalo roam.

33. **Bangkok** –
    Still the party city of Asia but for a more sophisticated crowd.

34. **The Jeseniky, Czech Republic** –
    Old World spa culture meets the budding ski scene.

35. **Waiheke, New Zealand** –
A homegrown art scene beckons from down under.

36. **Yucatán, Mexico** –
Whew! More time for culture and comfort.

37. **Charlevoix, Québec** –
A Cirque du Soleil fortune finances a train to the slopes.

38. **Pecs, Hungary** –
Cultures mesh in Hungary's "borderless city."

39. **Republic of Congo** –
The other Congo, Africa's newest safari destination.

40. **Ireland** –
The Emerald Isle reaches out with an ancestral celebration.

41. **Getaria, Spain** –
Fishing for design from a famed native son.

42. **Mergui Islands, Myanmar** –
Live-aboard diving on a remote archipelago.

43. **The Falkland Islands** –
Despite tensions, development at Britain's remote outpost.

44. **Washington, D.C.** –
A new food scene to welcome a renewed administration.

45. **Casablanca, Morocco** –
A city of cinematic fame has emerged as an art destination.

46. **Paris, France** –
Seine-side strolling, minus the traffic.

For the full article and write-ups for each destination, go to:

bit.ly/mb-1111

It need not be an exotic location, but leaving the beaten path and going on to a place you've never been to before will open up a whole new dimension in your life and add to your Life Balance.

Key Takeaways:

1. When planning your next trip, consider leaving the beaten path.

2. Before you travel, determine what you want to achieve for yourself, your partnership, your friends or family during your journey.

3. Get the most out of your trip and make it a new entry in the diary of your life.

3. Time Without Your Devices

 We all long for quality time with our partner, family and friends. This means a good conversation, enjoying each other's presence or even simply enjoying silence together.

The distractions however are plentiful and we've all seen groups of people with their individual devices out. These are teens hanging out together, colleagues during rare get-togethers, families or even couples having dinner out together—all occupied individually with their tablets, androids or gadgets.

Sadly, often it is the device in our hands that prevents quality time from happening. It blocks out the breaks between topics that are needed to get to what is below the surface; that elusive place where the magic in good conversations happens.

As our attention spans have shortened, many of us now expect constant stimulation, but if you pull out your device and check your inbox at every lull in the conversation, you will never find the next conversation to follow.

Here are three tips to overcome the temptation of your device:

1. Get used to focusing again. Our attention spans as a whole may have gradually decreased, still, force yourself to focus when you meet with people and to not wander off to your device.

2. Relearn to appreciate the single stimulus of just being with somebody. Many aspects of another person's company, including the conversation, the sharing of

thoughts and emotions, and even the periods of silence together, are enough stimulation all by themselves.

3. Be active in the conversation. Your life is exciting and your thoughts are interesting and sharing these bits with others is what keeps a conversation going. Contributing your part will also help you discover aspects and angles of your life you may not have considered.

Key Takeaways:

1. Focus on the presence of the people you spend time with. Fight the temptation to pull out your device every time the conversation slows down.

2. Appreciate the stimulus of just being with somebody. It seems straight-forward, but we sometimes forget that a friend, colleague, or family member can be a great source of insight, fun and wisdom all on their own.

3. Don't just be a consumer in a conversation— contribute to it. You are more interesting than you may think.

4. Plan Your Vacation Carefully

 Walking around the office muttering about project details gone wrong? Staring glassy-eyed at your computer screen without a coherent thought in your head? Trying to remember what direct sunlight feels like on your face? It's official—you need a vacation.

Even the most passionate workaholics need time off. Burnout is a risk in our relentlessly connected world, so take time to formally plan your time off to ensure you get a chance to unplug, unwind, and recharge:

- Create an annual vacation plan and request time off well in advance, e.g. toward the end of the current year for the next:
    - Communicate your plans early so that your team and other potentially impacted colleagues can schedule accordingly.
    - Align with colleagues when necessary to ensure everyone on your team has an opportunity to take time off when they would like to.
- Balance your own needs with the needs of your family and employer when making plans. Ideally, don't work during your vacation—the point is to rest and recharge:
    - Arrange coverage in advance with someone you trust to stand in for you and ensure your work is well documented so you don't have an anxiety attack during cocktail hour on the beach.

- Agree to an emergency contact method so that you don't have to check your work email every day to trust that all is well.

- Leave your smartphone at home—that's right, don't take it with you! Or, at the very least, deactivate work mail on it to resist the temptation to check in all the time. Depending on your level of enslavement, withdrawal symptoms shouldn't last long.

• All well and good, but what if …? You can drive yourself crazy with never-ending "what if" scenarios associated with taking time off, but here are a few you might find yourself experiencing and tips to counteract them:

- I simply cannot be disconnected or be away long enough for time off to be considered a "vacation." Ok, so just take a few days off here and there throughout the year or whatever time period you're planning for, but do yourself a favor and disconnect completely.

- Or, take that longer vacation, but plan to work X number of days or hours while you're on it—draw a boundary and don't cross it.

- Need to be at a work-related event that occurs during your planned vacation? Consider taking your vacation anyway and traveling to the event from your vacation location.

- Need to spend some time during your vacation time to catch-up on email so you're not buried with it when you get back to the office? Use the travel time back home to catch up using you device of choice to spare yourself the inevitably bad in-flight entertainment.

Use your creativity to find other ways to make this work—treat your time off as sacrosanct, you deserve it.

Please Note: Vacation policies vary from country to country. Check with your local HR team in advance to understand your specific rules regarding time off from work.

Key Takeaways:

1. Create an annual vacation plan and pencil in your time off well in advance.
2. While you're away, plan to have a "deputy" and an emergency contact method, etc. to give yourself peace of mind and keep you from checking to see if everything is ok all the time.
3. Be creative in making your vacation happen despite challenges.

5. On People Who Want to Be Unhappy

 You know the situation. Somebody you care about is unhappy and you want to help, yet that person pushes away any advice or help you offer. Their complaints are never-ending and being with them is more exasperating than anything.

 Surrounding yourself with people who want to be unhappy is not only frustrating, it's also counterproductive to your own pursuit for happiness. There might be a solution though to dealing with chronically unhappy people, and the first step is identifying and acknowledging the people who simply don't wish to be happy.

Diagnosing "Satisfied Unhappiness"

Here are three striking symptoms of chronically negative people:

1. Even in an overwhelmingly positive environment, they will focus on a negative. The evening is lush, the company is great, the atmosphere at the restaurant is wonderful, yet the first thing they say when dinner is served is "gosh, this portion is so small!"

2. Every encounter has a negative spin to it. The person who wants to be unhappy will manage to shed a negative light on to every story they tell. The people they met were ugly or unfriendly or just idiots. The work their colleagues did was incompetent, incomplete, and of low quality. The hotel they stayed at during their vacation was noisy, dirty, and had unfriendly staff.

3. Every offer for help will get rejected. As the person who enjoys being unhappy complains about various aspects of their life, you will try to come up with solutions, advice, and help. You will be surprised to see that every suggestion and offer gets rejected. There are many excuses as to why and you just don't seem to be able to help.

Of course, everybody has off days and all of us have most likely exhibited isolated incidents of these behaviors before. However, friends and acquaintances who frequently and consistently exhibit these patterns are another story. You may find yourself drained after meeting with them and seriously consider severing your friendship.

Withdrawal or Compassion?

It's up to you to decide on how you wish to deal with people who enjoy being unhappy. One thing you should not do however is let their toxic behavior drag you down. Constantly being shot down, or commiserating with negative people can pull you into a negative mindset too. (See the chapter on compassion and commiseration on page 55).

Your first option is to withdraw. If you find a person who enjoys being unhappy starting to bring you down, stay away! Focus on the people around you who want to enjoy life and live it to the fullest.

What if the other person is a family member or someone you care deeply about? In that case, you will have to cope with it, and that means understanding and acknowledging that the other person gets a certain satisfaction from their own negativity. Instead of trying to fix their problems, understand what that person needs when they complain: comfort, compassion, and friendship. You will find that your relationship with them will become much more relaxed and enjoyable, once you stop trying to find solutions to their problems and simply become a shoulder to cry on.

It can get difficult to listen to the same problems again and again and not offer solutions, but the art of understanding is knowing when to offer advice and when to simply listen.

Key Takeaways:

1. Identify the chronically negative people in your circles.
2. Determine if you would prefer to withdraw your friendship or to be compassionate with them.
3. If you decide to be compassionate, recognize that you can't fix their problems and enjoy the more relaxed relationship simply listening will bring you in the future.

6. Caring For Your Elderly Parents

 There is that milestone moment in life when the caring relationship between a parent and a child changes direction. This is when we start looking after our elderly parents. This is a situation that offers us a chance to give back, and in many families, it is also a situation with a lot of potential for stress, disappointment, and unnecessary anger.

Help, Love and Being Too Close

Regardless of how much you must actually do for your parents, there are usually three major concerns that must be addressed in a relationship between a child caring for an elderly parent.

Operational concerns include keeping the household running, and maintaining the parents' health through medical errands and activities.

Emotional concerns involve making sure the parents are not lonely, being active in their lives and helping maintain the general emotional health of everyone involved.

However, both of these concerns can quickly snowball into a third category of becoming overwhelmed. This means having to visit the parents every day, when before you visited a fraction of that time. It means doing things out of obligation or duty, not out of joy, and the guilty/resentful feelings that may arise from feeling obligated. This is being too close and it often leads to disappointments and frustration.

The Five Things to Do When Looking After Your Parents

To keep the situation healthy and pleasant, here are the five things you'll want to do when you look after your elderly parents:

Speak About Your Needs

Understand each other's operational and emotional requirements so that everyone's expectations are clear.

Know the Difference Between a Child and a Nurse

As a child you can give emotional support, and you will need emotional support—but there might be a physical component you are not ready or qualified to provide. Acknowledge when the physical side of caring for your parents starts taking a toll and let a professional take over.

Define Your Boundaries

Once your parents need more care and support, you will have to see them more, but you must decide how much time and energy you can commit. Define your boundaries and then clearly communicate them to your parents to avoid disappointment on both sides.

Get Help

If all of your time is getting consumed in operational support, see if you can find help so you can spend more quality time with your parents. Bring in the help of siblings or other family members—or if you can afford it, outsource some help by hiring someone to come clean, or to drive your parents to their appointments.

Take a Break

If you're starting to get irritated with each other, it's time for a break. Speak about alternatives that allow both you and your parents to maintain a healthy distance for a while so that you can enjoy each other's company again.

Key Takeaways:

1. Speak openly about your needs with your parents and understand theirs.
2. Try to remember that you're their child first, not just their nurse.
3. Define your boundaries. Don't take on more than you can handle.
4. Consider getting help if the operational support is starting to overwhelm you.
5. If you get short tempered with each other, it's time for a break.

7. Hands-Free Timesavers

  Have you ever considered equipping the main telephone you use in your home with a headset? Allowing yourself to have extended phone conversations with your hands-free will create amazing time-saving opportunities for you.

Think about tasks you must regularly perform but that do not require your full mental capacity. This can be preparing a meal or doing laundry. If you feel that you're lacking the time to maintain your relationship with friends or family members, then getting into the habit of using these tasks for a catch-up phone call may be a wonderful solution to your problem.

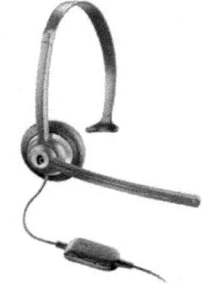

Phone headsets come in all shapes and sizes. They are usually pretty affordable and the system depends on the connectivity your phone offers. Whichever headset you choose, it should be comfortable, offer good sound quality for yourself and the person you speak with, and allow you to move freely while being on the phone.

Amazon Link

Here is a sample link to one of the headsets I prefer.
bit.ly/mb-3003

Key Takeaways:

1. See if you can think of any tasks in your home or in your car that do not require your full mental capacity.
2. Get a headset for your phone.
3. Use this time to catch-up on the phone with your friends and family.

8. The Five Essential Truths About Friendship

Friends are one of the most important ingredients to our happiness, and yet at the same time we may find ourselves wondering what exactly happened when things go wrong. Here are five essential truths to keep in mind about friendship:

1. Proximity Doesn't Matter

In this day and age, friends don't need to live in the same city or even in the same country anymore. Travel, periods of our life abroad, and people from other nations coming into our lives give us the opportunity to experience close friendships all around the globe. Today's means of communication make it easy to stay in touch and remain friends.

2. Frequency Doesn't Matter

Some friendships require regular connection; others can last through long periods of no communication. While being connected through social networks like Facebook might help us see what our friends are up to, there are situations where friends meet after years of not hearing from each other and picking up right where they left off.

3. Unequal Effort Can Work

Some people are really bad at staying in touch. They are bad networkers, lazy letter writers, they don't remember to call, and just don't seem to have time for the friends in their life. As annoying as that may be, they might also be wonderful people who enjoy every moment once you actually get together. Try to accept as a fact of life that in many friendships, one side will invest more effort to stay in touch than the other.

4. Unequal Affection Doesn't Work

Friendships grow between people who mutually like each other and enjoy each other's company. Sometimes this feeling of affection is unequally distributed amongst those involved. Above, we learned that unequal effort might have nothing to do with the amount of affection in a friendship, but friendships based in unequal affection usually do not last long. (And it is generally easy to determine who has the stronger feelings.)

5. You Win Some, You Lose Some

As we progress through life, we meet new people and some become close enough to be called friends. At the same time we lose sight of other friends until one day we have to admit that we are no longer friends... and that's okay.

While life-long relationships are the invaluable diamonds in the world of friendship, there are also friends for certain phases of your life. Those who were our best friends in elementary school, high school, college, or our first job might not always be the important people in our lives. As long as we don't lose friends for the wrong reasons (see the Five Essential Things to Maintain Friendships on page 162) accept that some of your friends will exit your life at some point.

Understanding and accepting these five essential truths about friendship will make it easier for you to grow and maintain your circle of friends.

Key Takeaways:

1. Don't shy away from maintaining friendships around the globe.

2. Accept unequal effort to maintain a friendship, but don't accept unequal affection.

3. Check out "The Five Essential Things to Maintain Friendships" (see page 162) to make sure you're not losing friends for the wrong reasons.

9. How to Make New Friends

Six important tips to expand and maintain your social circles

Our friends are an important part of our lives and play a key role in our Life Balance. Quite naturally, friends will come and go during our lives. As we try to surround ourselves with people who share our values and interests, we see that friends can help us become the person we want to be.

Meeting new people can seem random at times, but it is for good reason that the process of establishing new social relationships is called "making" friends. We can have an active role in the process by contributing some planning and energy. Here are some proven tips on how to make and keep your friends.

1. Make It Your Focus and Priority

Most of us live lives within a rigid framework of routine: time at work, time with the family, shopping and errands. This leaves few opportunities to meet new people. If you've decided that meeting new people is a priority for you, you'll have to make it your focus and actively start the process, as it will most likely not happen accidentally.

2. Start with Social Media

Social networks like Facebook are not only good for keeping in touch with existing friends around the globe, they can also offer access to regional groups focused around common interests. With all these online platforms, finding interesting people around you has never been easier. Check to see if you can find a group in your neighborhood, at your kids' school, something involving your hobby, or a group centered around local art or live performances. See who is active in these groups and participate in the discussions that interest you. Don't be too shy to be the first to suggest moving the virtual acquaintance into the real world. A tailgate party for the next game, or drinks together after the concert you will all be attending. If you are into sports, suggesting to run or workout together is also a good start.

3. Places in the Real World

If you want to meet new people in real life, you'll most likely have to divert from your routine. Sign up for any sort of fitness class or go to the gym rather than working out at home. Attend a public reading if you enjoy literature, or join a theater workshop if you're into performing arts. If you have any sort of hobby or interest, try to find a public place to pursue it with likeminded people: an art class, craft circle, hiking group, sports team, or choir are all excellent opportunities to quickly find people who share at least one interest with you. Whenever you find yourself in a new group, be open and approachable and talk to the other people you find there. Listen to what they have to say and pick the individuals you'd like to get to know better.

4. From Sight to Small Talk to Connecting

Though it seems pretty straightforward, it does take some practice to start a conversation with someone who looks interesting. Asking advice on how things work is always a good start. You can then ask questions about the other person and listen actively to what they have to say. Following up on topics that sound interesting can potentially unearth commonalities between the two of you. Communicate your interest with statements like "I am new in town and I'm looking for someone to work out with." If you think that the person has the potential to become a friend, don't hesitate to suggest an activity. Something like "hey, you seem to have the same attitude towards ... as I; would you like to go for coffee after next week's session?" is a good way of showing your interest in getting to know the other person better.

5. Put Effort into Planning Things

Living an active social life doesn't happen accidentally. It takes planning that somebody has to do. All too often, friends lose sight of each other because nobody takes ownership for organizing the next get together. So look out for events that might be fun to attend together; new bars and restaurants that sound great to try; an interesting show or exhibition coming to town, or just a bottle of wine you'd like to enjoy with some friends. Don't be afraid to be the one to reach out and suggest getting together for these things.

In an ideal world, planning joint activities is equally distributed amongst friends, but in reality, everyone has different abilities, strengths and weaknesses. If organizing events is your strength, this is something you can contribute to your friends.

6. Stay in Touch

During our life we'll find wonderful people who stay only for a particular stretch, like our time in college or a trip to India. Other friends are such great fits that the friendship can last a lifetime. These friendships are amongst the greatest gifts in life so make some effort to sustain them. Use technology to bridge geographical distance; use social networks to connect and stay in touch about the little things in life. If you need reminders, put them into your calendar. For example, if you send out Christmas cards, maintain a list to not forget anyone and potentially add a write-up of how your year went for those friends you don't connect with often during the year.

When you travel, keep your eyes open for small and interesting things to bring back for your good friends, or surprise them while you're gone by sending something as old-fashioned as a real postcard. If you are in an extraordinary location or experience something awesome and you wish your best friend was there with you—call them and let them know!

As you can see, finding and maintaining good friends is something you can plan for. Considering how valuable friends are in our lives, the time and effort you put into this are well worth the investment.

Key Takeaways:

1. Realize that meeting new people is often NOT a matter of chance. If you want or need new friends, don't wait for it to happen. Make a conscious effort.

2. Use social network sites to connect to people around you—use classes or local events exploring your interests or hobbies to meet others with similar interests.

3. Friendships need maintenance. Use technology to keep in contact and don't be afraid to be the first one to suggest a get together or the first one to reach out.

10. The Five Essential Things to Maintain Friendships

Friends are like a collection of valuable gems in our life. They are all precious and beautiful for a different reason. We don't want to lose any of them, which is why maintaining friendships is a skill that contributes significantly to our Life Balance. Here are the five essential tips for maintaining the friendships in your life.

1. Plan For It!

Depending on how many friends you have, maintaining them can be quite an organizational challenge. Make reaching out to your friends an ongoing element of your week. Find moments to reach out to a friend for a good conversation on the phone, like during your afternoon commute or while ironing your clothes. (See chapter on page 154)

Make good use of modern tools like Skype for free calls with your friends abroad, or WhatsApp for casual exchanges on the go, but keep in mind the good old-fashioned postcard as a very personal greeting from places you visit.

To not miss any of your friends, consider maintaining a list on which you track when you last made contact. Put your friends' birthdays into your calendar and let them hear from you on that day.

For staying in touch and sharing about your life around the holidays, consider a longer email with a photo attached rather than a standard greeting card. This will also allow you to reach out to more friends while spending less time on the task.

2. Give More, Expect Less

When you maintain a friendship, you invest your time, your effort, and your emotions. When you meet your friends you engage in meaningful conversations. You listen, you are engaged in your friend's story, and you ask questions. As we saw in the "Five Essential Truths About Friendship" (see page 155), the effort in a friendship is not always equally distributed. Keeping that in mind, invest yourself only in the people who are really important to you. Do things for your friends because it causes you joy, not because you expect invitations or gestures back from them and you will enjoy the effort you make that much more.

3. Live and Let Live

All of our friends are different and the older we get, the more difficult it might seem to accept these differences. In school or college it might have seemed more possible to hang out with people considerably different from yourself and still have a good time. Try to maintain this generous flexibility even as you grow older and cultivate friendships with people who are different from you. It helps to find the common ground with each friend. Some may be great to go out with, others are ideal workout partners and the next kind will always be there for you if you need help. Remember that you don't always have to agree on deep profound values with someone to have a good time with them.

4. Though Sometimes It Helps to Share Values

It's important to have friends who offer different backgrounds and situations, and to remember to relax and kick back with a more casual approach to friendship. However, on the other extreme is the situation when you realize you have a lot of friends for casual going out or fun activities—but not a lot of friends to confide in, or friends whom you could really depend on and trust. If fair-weather friends are getting you down, acknowledge that you have only a limited amount of time and resources and try to focus on a handful of dependable friends rather than twenty shallow ones.

5. Social Media and Friendship

Having hundreds of friends on Facebook doesn't necessarily mean that you have a healthy and valuable ecosystem of true friends. However, social networks like Facebook are still valuable helpers for maintaining your friendships. Sharing the little events in your life online allows you to start the conversation with your friends at a more profound level once you see them again. Because they've kept track of what has happened since you last met, you can dive into the details, feelings, and emotions immediately.

Try to keep your list of "friends" crisp and short on Facebook. If you don't want to reject anyone, consider creating a group for your real friends and limiting your posts to that group. Also, separate your friends from your work environment. Choose one social network like Facebook for your friends and another one like LinkedIn for your business contacts.

Your life is complex enough. Focus your energy and effort on the quality of the time you have with your friends, not on the operations around it. Try meeting your friends more often in a casual environment, rather than staging formal dinner invitations; balance casual relaxed friendships with deeper, profound ones, and use tools such as email and Skype to reach out to more friends with less effort.

Following these five steps will allow you to focus on the quality of time spent together rather than the complexity of the organizational framework.

Key Takeaways:

1. Give more. Expect less.
2. Use social media to organize and maintain your friendships.
3. Accept that some of your friendships may be based in simply enjoying an activity together rather than deep agreement—but don't forget the profound friendships you can really count on.
4. Focus on the quality of time together rather than the organizational framework.

11. Tools for Staying in Touch

You read the chapter on the "Five Essential Things to Maintain Friendships" (see page 162). Here, we'll take a look at the tools that help us stay in touch with our friends, no matter where they are in the world.

How It Improves Your Life Balance

- By helping you stay up to date with the minutiae in your friends' lives, Facebook helps pick up the conversation at a more profound level when you meet again. Keep in mind:
    - Limit your "friends" on Facebook to the friends you really want to stay in touch with.
    - Ideally, have the business equivalent for Facebook (for example LinkedIn), so that you can keep Facebook for your private contacts.
    - If you feel obligated to accept all friendship requests, create a group for your real friends and limit your postings to those.
    - Go through your privacy settings and make sure your posts are only visible to your friends.
    - Your starting point: Facebook.com

- Skype allows you to chat with, speak to, and see your friends, free of charge.
    - It's great for staying in touch with friends around the globe.

- With a webcam and a solid Internet connection, you can see each other.
- Skype is also available for your mobile, however, some carriers block you from using Skype for free phone calls. That still leaves you with a very useful chat functionality.
- Your starting point: Skype.com

- WhatsApp is great for day-to-day chat with sharing photos.
  - It has already replaced a huge part of the global SMS traffic.
  - There is no character limit.
  - It's also great for sharing a snapshot with a friend.
  - It is however currently only available for mobile phones.
  - It tells you which of your contacts in your address book also use WhatsApp.
  - Your starting point: search for WhatsApp in the app store on your mobile.
- Viber brings you the best of both worlds.
  - It has all the cool features of WhatsApp plus the free calls you can make with Skype.
  - Also works on a PC.
  - Your starting point: viber.com

You can find all of the apps above in the app store for your operating system.

Use it to:

1. Share the little things in your life. That way, when you meet again you can spend less time catching up and dive right into the conversation.

2. Save money while staying in touch with your friends around the world.

3. Create a space for true friends.

Part 4 Life Balance Advice for Your Work

1. Reduce Your Worklist

 Is your work list in the office getting longer and longer? Have tasks been sneaking onto that list for years? Unfortunately, these lists can be like attics and sheds—things get in there and they tend to stay. Bring the concept of spring cleaning to your work and see if you can clean out unnecessary tasks from your list to save some time.

Who Benefits from Your Work?

It might seem like an odd question, but an important one to consider. The most obvious answer is that your work should benefit your employer. The company will either benefit from your innovation when you create new ideas or concepts, or see its established processes being maintained when you operate within predefined precepts. So if it's your employer  who benefits from your innovation and maintenance, what is the benefit for you?

Beyond monetary compensation, your work should bring you reputation and satisfaction–ideally both. A task can add to your reputation if your good work gets noticed. A task can also add to your satisfaction if it's something you're good at and that you thoroughly enjoy doing.

The Task-Benefit Matrix

With the task benefiting either your employer or yourself we can position it on the matrix in Figure 6:

Be a Superman

To get into the desired Superman quadrant, you should focus on tasks that equally benefit your employer as well as yourself. This is the area where you're making a real contribution and enjoying yourself in the process. After a day spent in this quadrant you go home feeling energized, satisfied, and proud of what you have achieved.

Don't Be a Slave

Some employers might also be drawn to the top left quadrant where they see equal benefit in terms of innovation or maintenance. However, your benefit here is minimal. Work in this quadrant drains your energy rather than providing positive stimulus. After a day spent on work in this quadrant you may go

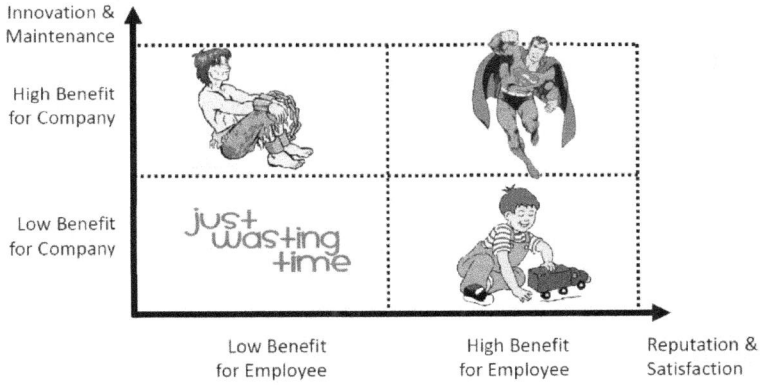

Figure 6: The Task-Benefit Matrix

home feeling happy for what you have contributed to your company, but you will be tired, frustrated, and drained of energy, which probably doesn't make you a fun person to spend the evening with.

Tasks that add a lot of benefit to your company and little to yourself should not be on your task list. You should either delegate these tasks to others in your organization who ideally enjoy these tasks much more or are better suited to perform them. Alternatively, consider outsourcing these tasks to vendors.

Don't Play Around

In the bottom right quadrant you find tasks that benefit you, but contribute very little to your company. One example of tasks in this area are so-called pet tasks, functions you perform well and enjoy doing, but which are not in line with your current level in the organization anymore. You need to let go of these by delegating them downwards in your team. They do provide benefit to your company, but you are definitely the wrong person to perform them.

If the task you thoroughly enjoy adds no benefit to your company, it's a hobby. Don't do it at work.

Don't Waste Time

The bottom left quadrant on our chart is the black hole of wasting time. Tasks performed here benefit neither your employer nor yourself. Maintaining overly bureaucratic processes are one example. Surfing the web beyond what is needed for research or a short break is another. Several surveys estimate that the amount of time wasted at work is between five and ten percent. Eliminate the tasks that fall into this quadrant to free up time you need for improving your Life Balance.

Now that you have cleaned up your work list, make sure it doesn't clog up again. Mark time in your calendar regularly; say once every six months, to repeat this spring cleaning and keep your work list well-defined and crisp.

Key Takeaways:

1. Reflect on your work list regularly using the Task Benefit Matrix.
2. Take action to eliminate tasks that fall into quadrants two (slaving), three (playing around) and four (wasting time) from your work list.

2. Decide When and Where You Work!

 Delivering high-quality work anytime, anywhere in our untethered world is simply a part of life now—let's face it, most of us no longer work a set number of hours in a single location, and this modern reality can be both a blessing and a curse at times.

In many modern occupations we are assessed on the quality rather than on just the quantity of our work. The flexibility many of us enjoy of working anytime, anywhere can contribute to that quality, but striking a balance between always "on" and knowing when to disconnect is one of the keys to balance.

Ask yourself the questions below to help you understand how to get the maximum efficiency out of the work flexibility your employer might offer you.

- Is there one best place for me to work—in the office or in my home office, or some combination of the two?

- Which location helps me maximize efficiency and productivity?

- Can I work from home? Will my manager support and enable that choice? Does my work lend itself to that option?

- If I chose to work from home exclusively, will I miss the face-to-face social interaction that I have with my colleagues in the office?

- If I have to work in the office, what other options are available to foster creativity and recharge my batteries when I need energy?

- Can I take a walk during work time to help stimulate creativity and think up the new process or solution?

- Can we create an area in the office where I can sit and talk with coworkers in an informal way that encourages and makes it fun to collaborate?

- Am I equipped with the proper technology to allow me to work anywhere and be productive? Smartphone, tablet, Skype, etc.?

Refer to our related advice on gadgets for remote (see page 50) and virtual collaboration (see page 217) to help you pick the right tools for staying in touch.

Check out your employer's programs to enhance flexible work.

Many employers recognize and support the need for balance between work and personal matters and believe that flexibility is an essential element to promoting an engaged, efficient, and productive work environment.

In support of these beliefs your employer may have a ready-to-use program to provide flexible work options for its employees. Check with your HR team to find out if such a program is in place.

Key Takeaways:

1. Determine to what extent your work could be done from flexible locations and during flexible hours.
2. Understand your employer's guidelines and preferences to build your personal plan.
3. Choose the right balance of locations, times, and tools to find the best mix to support your Life Balance.

3. 15 Things to Work Smarter

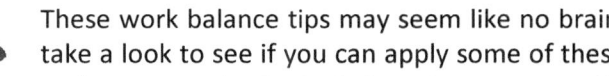

These work balance tips may seem like no brainers, but take a look to see if you can apply some of these simple and necessary tactics to help reduce your workload and stress, and have more fun at your job:

Roles and Responsibilities (R&R)

Do you have a clear understanding of what your job responsibilities are, what your deliverables include, and what your manager, team, and organization's expectations are? If not, then take control and work with your manager to ensure your R&Rs are clearly spelled out:

1. Define your R&Rs to avoid duplication.
2. Use a responsibility assignment model like DACI or RACI to help you clarify your role (bit.ly/mb-5003).
3. Adjust your R&Rs over time and ensure you and your manager are aligned and you both understand the associated expectations.

Timing

4. Make sure you have realistic timelines and expectations.
5. Build time into your calendar to think and recover—a good way to do this is to use an "email free" day to review the week's work, prepare for the next week, and spend time on your own development as well as new ideas.

Mingle

6. Take breaks during your work days/weeks and make them social—spend time with your peers and colleagues to energize yourself, bounce ideas off of them, and find out what's happening in other parts of your team or organization.

Work Smarter, Not Harder

7. Prioritize, prioritize, prioritize.
8. Learn to say no! You can't do everything, so be strategic about the tasks you take on.
9. If your department budget allows for it, consider using service partners more than before to scale you workload.
10. Reflect on work items regularly and cancel the ones that aren't on the "A" list.
11. Identify and break bad habits.
12. Attractive and fun as they may sound, don't take on pet tasks that are incompatible with your role.
13. Accept that at the end of the day there will always be more work to do.
14. Look for training and educational opportunities supported by your organization that can add knowledge and skills to will help you in your role and advance your expertise.
15. Everyone has more work than they can manage at times, so share your favorite tips and tricks with your friends and colleagues on how to cut the fat from your work day.

Key Takeaways:

1. Review the list above and pick a few items that apply to you.

2. Make a point of trying these items out over the next few weeks.

4. Delegate

Your list of deliverables seems overwhelming. At the end of the day, there are too many uncompleted tasks. You have too many things on your plate and you can't do it all yourself. If you can relate to this scenario, you know it can make work a drag. You think, if only you had help. The truth is, you do, but you have to ask.

Learning to ask for help or delegating is easier said than done for some of us—we want to feel in control of our work and know that we can do it all ourselves. If this sounds like you, then incorporating delegation may be an important tactic in how you approach your work.

Check out the suggestions below to explore ways to incorporate delegation in your quest to better balance your work life.

Take Time to Delegate

Sometimes, it is easier to just dive in and do the work yourself than to plan effective delegation. However, once you make the decision to do it and have provided the necessary details to your delegate, you may be excited by how much time you win back and how much your delegate appreciates the opportunity.

Delegate with Confidence

No one works in a vacuum. Creativity requires collaboration and delegating to direct reports, team members, and peers facilitates creativity, success, and balance. The rewards of delegating can be great, so take the risk and do it—it creates trust, and helps build teams and relationships

Don't Be Shy

Keep in mind that delegating does not necessarily mean you're burdening your colleagues—they may actually love the challenge. Most people rise to the level of expectation you put on them, so delegate without fear. Remember to challenge your team members, and raise the level of complexity and potential over time to give team members the opportunity to shine.

Teamwork

Delegating is a necessary part of project work: no one can do it all alone. Project success most often depends on teamwork, and delegation can be a critical component of any work endeavor.

Delegation Readiness

Keep the delegation readiness of the person to whom you delegate in mind. Depending on their experience they might just need a clear objective like "give team ABC an update on our strategy for this year." A junior delegate may need more guidance and even have steps explained within the tasks in order to be successful. As such, delegation is also a great teaching opportunity to further develop your team members.

Key Takeaways:

1. Take the time to delegate. While it might seem faster to just do it yourself, this tactic will not be sustainable over time.

2. Don't be shy in delegating—what might seem burdensome to you could be the next exciting challenge for the team member to whom you delegate.

3. Keep the delegation readiness of the person to whom you delegate in mind. Be very specific about the objective and open about how to get there, as appropriate.

5. Make Sure You Like Your Work

 Do you like your work? Not everyone does all the time, of course, but the most fundamental prerequisite for balancing work in your life is that you like what you do. Otherwise, unhappiness is a given and balance elusive.

We recommend that you think about your Career Compass to determine where you are and where you want to go in your career. For your Career Compass, think about the two to five attributes your work must have for you to like it. For example:

- Want to make an impact and make full use of my skills and experience
- Must be fulfilling and allow me to shine
- Must be challenging
- Must work with nice people
- Must have flexibility in terms of when and where I work
- Must have opportunities for development and advancement
- Must work close to my kid's school so I can be there on time to pick her up
- Must work in the same city where my mother lives so that I can take care of her

Choose and/or create the attributes you pick for your compass, but keep the list as high-level and short as possible. For example:

- Limit your list of attributes to two to five—this is a good starting point and you can re-adjust as needed over time.

- Make your attributes general rather than too specific. Don't say "I want to become manager of the Finance team here at ACME Inc." unless you have a burning desire to do so and it's the only thing in work that will make you happy forever.

Use your compass to asses...

- ... how happy you are in your current job and what you need to change to be happier. Do you need to change the way you work in your current role, or even change jobs?
- ... new opportunities offered to you. They may sound tempting, but if they don't match your compass, they may lure you into a new situation that ultimately makes you unhappy. Additionally, new roles that you would not have considered—with the help of your Career Compass—might suddenly become a real option because they meet your key requirements for work satisfaction.

Finding a job that is a perfect fit may take time. Sometimes it takes courage to make a change, but when you find something that excites and motivates you, the rewards can be tremendous and ultimately outweigh the risks of the change.

Key Takeaways:

1. Define your own Career Compass with 3-5 attributes your work must fulfill.
2. Evaluate your current work situation using your Career Compass and use it to vet new opportunities.
3. Make changes when needed. Life is too short to do work you don't like.

6. Dealing with Email: Manage the Flood

 Please note: Before your start, please confirm that these suggestions align with your employer's IT policies to avoid any hassle.

Love it or hate it, it's become impossible to live without email and if you're not careful, your inbox can morph into a massive black hole that will suck the time and energy right out of you.

For many of us, one of the biggest contributors to overall workload has become managing email and the task can make you less productive at best and a little crazy at worst.

For anyone who has thought along these lines:

- I'm drowning in a flood of emails every day.
- If only I could find a way to manage the flood.
- Why do people CC me on everything?
- Microsoft really should eliminate the 'reply all' option,

I have developed this approach of dealing with email that will take about two hours to implement and a few days to get used to. Once in place, **this system will save you 15-60 minutes of email management every day**, time you may better invest elsewhere.

Here is an overview of the five steps (each step is further explained in the following chapters).

Step 1: Tuning Your Spam Engine

You will start to block emails you no longer wish to receive instead of deleting them.

Time saved: If twenty emails get sifted directly to the spam folder without you having to look at them, that saves you five seconds of figuring out 'is that spam?' for each email.

That means 1.5 minutes saved daily or 5.5 hours saved yearly.

See page 186 for the details.

Step 2: CCs Go Separate

CC-ed email means information you are meant to be aware of, but not necessarily react to. If not managed properly, these emails do have a way of cluttering up an inbox.

You will direct emails on which you are CC-ed to a designated folder to keep your inbox neater and more relevant.

Time saved: Thirty minutes per week by being able to focus on the most pertinent content in your inbox and dealing with the CC folder only twice per week **means one hundred hours saved per year.**

See page 188 for the details.

Step 3: Stop Using (Most) Folders

You will start to archive every (!) email that you receive. Also, you will no longer file emails in folders (some exceptions apply), but in quarterly archives, with a search engine that will help you find emails much faster than before.

You will observe your work style and then create a very limited number of folders that help you be more efficient.

Time saved: 150 mails per day times five seconds of thinking time to decide where to file it per email equals 12.5 minutes saved per day. **That's forty hours a year, or an entire work week!**

See page 190 for the details.

Step 4: Know Your Device

Make use of down time by using a hand held device for email.

Now that you have completed steps one to three, you can be a wizard on your device. Whenever you have time to kill; at the airport, at the dentist or on a train to work, use your device to read emails and delete them without having to worry about archiving or relocating to the right folder. Read your CC folder by glancing at the emails that were sent to you and delete them since you know that they have already been auto-archived.

Time saved: Twenty minutes per day that would otherwise have to happen in front of your PC means 1.5 hours per week or **300 hours per year.**

See page 195 for the details.

Step 5: Work with Your Admin (if you have one)

Move mails that can be handled by your admin, assistant or teammate into a dedicated, shared folder and agree to check this folder regularly. Grant your admin access to your inbox and have them help you fight the flood of emails. Forget about the times when you had to check email every day while being on vacation. Instead, have your admin cover for you while you are out.

Time saved: 15 minutes saved per day, meaning **fifty hours saved per year.**

See page 197 for the details.

Implementing all of the steps above can **easily free up to one hour per day** that you can now invest for more important things.

Key Takeaways:

1. Review the steps above and determine which of them apply to you. Rather choose too many than too few.

2. Find the detailed descriptions for each of the selected steps and add them to your selection.

3. Implement the steps that apply to you and give yourself a few days to get used to the new system– I am sure that you will be highly pleased with the results.

7. Dealing with Email: Tune Your Spam Engine

Please note: Before your start, please confirm that these suggestions align with your employer's IT policies to avoid any hassle.

Tuning Your Spam Engine

You will start to block emails you no longer wish to receive instead of just deleting them.

Benefits:

1. Rather than using the tedious unsubscribe link in suspicious newsletters (which often only reconfirms your email address for further spamming) you now use your spam engine to block these emails from getting to you in the future.

2. Over time, this will increase the number of emails that automatically go to your spam folder every day, easily cutting around 2-5 minutes of work out of your day. That's a full 1-2 working days per year!

Do It Now:

1. Prominently position the "Block" button next to your "Delete" button.
2. Make it a habit to block rather than delete unwanted email.

3. Make it a habit to block rather than unsubscribe from emails your no longer want to receive; it is much faster and avoids reconfirming your email address to dubious senders for further spamming.
4. Every now and then, create a backup of your junk mail settings. This way you can take your trained spam engine with you, if you switch computers in the future.

Time saved: If twenty emails get sifted directly to the spam folder without you having to look at them, that saves you five seconds of figuring out 'is that spam?' for each email. That means 1.5 minutes saved daily or 5.5 hours saved yearly.

Links:

How to add the 'block' button to your ribbon in Outlook:

bit.ly/mb-5007

Key Takeaways:

1. Prominently position the 'Block' button next to your 'Delete' button.
2. Make it a habit to block rather than delete unwanted email.
3. Make it a habit to block rather than unsubscribe from emails your no longer want to receive; it is much faster and avoids reconfirming your email address to dubious senders for further spamming.

8. Dealing with Email: CCs Go Separate

 Please note: Before your start, please confirm that these suggestions align with your employer's IT policies to avoid any hassle.

 If you're receiving too many emails during your day, try to separate the less important ones to keep your inbox looking trim. Here is one way to do that in Outlook:

Separate Your CC Email from Your Inbox

Direct mails on which you are only CC-ed to a designated folder to keep the contents of your inbox neater and more relevant.

Benefits:

- By keeping CC-ed emails out of your inbox, you'll be able to see and address personally relevant emails much more efficiently.

- You can now use idle time (such as commuting time) more effectively by looking at your CC-ed emails, which generally only require reading and deleting. The emails will all be together now, an additional benefit of auto archiving (described on page 190).

Do It Now:

1. Create a new folder in your Outlook called 'CC Emails.'

2. Create a rule in your Outlook to redirect mails you are only CC-ed on to this new 'CC Emails' folder.

   Note, when defining the rule, make it a condition that

a. *you are on the 'CC' line of the email you want to move to the new folder **AND***

b. *you are not on the 'TO' line of that particular email. This way you will not move an email that started out as an issue going back and forth in a thread for a while with you on the CC, now ultimately addressed directly to you.*

3. Inform your colleagues that you will look at your CC-ed emails only every few days or so from now on and that they need to address an email to you directly if they expect an immediate reaction or reply from you.

Time saved: Thirty minutes per week by being focused on your inbox and dealing with the CC folder only twice per week means one hundred hours saved per year.

Links:

How to create a new folder in Outlook:

bit.ly/mb-5008a

How to create a rule in Outlook:

bit.ly/mb-5008b

Key Takeaways:

1. Create a new folder in your Outlook called 'CC Emails.'

2. Create a rule in your Outlook that redirects any email you are CC-ed on to this new folder.

3. Only manage this folder (your less important inbox) twice a week.

9. Dealing with Email: Stop Using (Most) Folders

(TIME SAVER)

Please note: Before your start, please confirm that these suggestions align with your employer's IT policies to avoid any hassle.

From Folders to Quarterly Filing

If you open your Outlook program and go to your email, you might see that you use a very elaborate system of folders to file all incoming mail.

Creating such a system of folders has probably cost you a lot of effort. Maintaining it and properly filing your email into these folders will cost you even more time which means it might be ready for some drastic steps. As crazy as it might sound, if you follow me through this step three, step by step, you will  save up to a full working week per year in sorting and retrieving your email from the folder system you have been using so far.

Here is how you do it: Stop filing your emails in folders. Instead of having to go through reading an email, thinking of where to file it and then moving it to a folder, you potentially have a much faster way of dealing with your email and even of improving the reliability of your archiving. Let's explore how to do this in Outlook:

From folder Filing to Quarterly Filing

You will start to archive every (!) email that you receive. Also, you will no longer file emails in folders (some exceptions apply), but in quarterly archives, with a search engine that will help you find emails much faster than before.

You will observe your work style and then create a very limited number of folders that help you be more efficient.

Benefits:

1. You'll save around 5-10 seconds per email thinking about which folder to save it to or whether or not to delete the email. At 150 emails per day, this is 10-15 minutes saved every day.

2. With every email being auto-archived, your inbox is now your to-do list. Use unproductive time in your day (waiting for a bus or at the doctor's office) to read email on your handheld and delete them after you read them. See the dedicated chapter on how to fully take advantage of dead time on page 195.

Do It Now:

1. Create a folder named 'archive' in your mail file.

2. Create a rule that copies every incoming mail into the 'archive' folder immediately after it arrives.

3. Use your Outlook search feature or install a mail search program (e.g. copernic.com) to speed up your search for archived mail.

Now you...

- ... can use your inbox as a to-do list: every email gets deleted after you are done with it, since you already have a copy in your archive folder.

- ... no longer have to spend 5-10 seconds per email to determine whether to keep it, where to file it and moving it there. That's already 10-15 minutes saved every day or 2-7 hours every month if you receive a hundred or so emails a day.

- ... can go through your emails much faster on your hand-held if you use one. No more moving to folders—just read and delete.

- ... can move the emails from your archive folder to an Outlook data file (.pst) every now and then to keep your email file small. I create a new .pst file for every quarter.

- ... can use your search program to not only find emails but also documents on your PC when you're looking something up.

Folders to Keep

You will observe your work style and then create a very limited number of folders to help you be more efficient. The following are examples that may or may not apply to you.

Benefit:

- Some frequent tasks related to your incoming email lend themselves to use folders in Outlook. This way you can group, delay or monitor events for more efficiency.

- Moving emails from your inbox to a folder will keep your inbox concise and relevant—remember, it's now your to-do list!

- You can delete emails from your folders once they are no longer needed—a benefit of you now using auto archiving.

- Time savings from this exercise are difficult to estimate, but they can be significant if you are able to delegate more efficiently or have a quick destination for emails from your inbox without having to use a complex flagging or task management system.

Do It Now:

1. Create folders you need called '***foldername' and have them appear at the top of your folder list.

2. For your most used folders, consider creating a quick task to allow you to move emails at the click of a button.

3. Examples of folders to be used:

    a. ***Print

    For emails that have content or attachments you want to print out next time you have access to a printer.

    b. ***Waiting for

    For emails that relate to events in the future you want to monitor, e.g. order confirmations until the goods are received, task delegations until the employee has completed the task, requests for information until such information is received.

    c. ***YourAdmin'sName

    Give your admin access to this folder and agree that every email therein is for them to address. Moving mails to this folder is the fastest way of delegating tasks that don't require explanation. See the special chapter on this item on page 197.

Time Saved:

100-150 emails per day times 5-10 seconds of thinking time regarding where to file it equals 8-25 minutes saved a day, or **25-85 hours saved per year.**

Links:

How to create a new folder in Outlook:

bit.ly/mb-5008a

How to create a rule in Outlook:

bit.ly/mb-5008b

Key Takeaways:

1. Move from many project or topic related email folders to one folder per quarter.
2. Copy every incoming email into your one archive folder automatically.
3. Use Outlook's search or a search tool like Copernic.com to search for emails when you need to find them.

10. Dealing with Email: Know Your Device

Please note: Before your start, please confirm that these *suggestions align with your employer's IT policies to avoid any hassle.*

Making the Best of Dead Time by Using a Handheld Device for Email

 Now that you have completed steps one to three, you can be a wizard on your smartphone, tablet or android. Whenever you have spare time (at the airport, at the dentist or on a train to work), you can

1. Use your device to read email, and immediately delete them without having to worry about archiving it or moving it to the right folder.

2. Read your CC folder by glancing at the emails that were sent to you only for your information and delete them efficiently since you know they have already been auto-archived for you.

Time Saved:

Twenty minutes per day that would otherwise have to happen in front of your PC means 1.5 hours per week or 300 hours per year.

Key Takeaways:

1. Get a handheld device, i.e. a smart phone or tablet, and configure it to receive your work email.

2. Use it during dead time to read and delete your email (since you set-up auto-archiving in step three of this series, you don't have to worry about deleting something important).

3. Make sure to leave your devices off though during quality time with your family or your friends (see page 143).

11. Dealing with Email: Working with Your Admin

Please note: Before your start, please confirm that these suggestions align with your employer's IT policies to avoid any hassle.

A Shared Folder for Your Admin

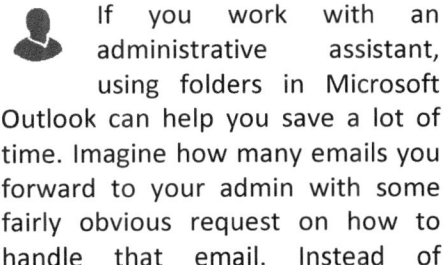 If you work with an administrative assistant, using folders in Microsoft Outlook can help you save a lot of time. Imagine how many emails you forward to your admin with some fairly obvious request on how to handle that email. Instead of forwarding each and every time, create a folder in your Outlook account and give your admin access to that particular folder. Agree to have your admin check the content of this folder several times a day. Now, rather than forwarding an email to your admin with the request to handle this particular message, simply move the email into the newly created folder. As per your agreement, your admin will know what to do.

Setting up a system like this not only saves you time; in many cases, it can enrich the work for your admin, since this delegation adds more responsibility to his or her work.

Granting Full Access to Your Inbox

Another great way of collaborating with your admin on email is granting access to your email inbox. Your admin can now help you deal with the daily flow of incoming email by simply taking action on that particular message and then deleting it.

Remember, all the email has been set up for automatic archiving in a previous step of this process (see page 190).

Involving your admin in your daily email management will likely create a new level of trust and expose your admin to a wider scope of your work. As a result, they will be much better able to support you in your daily work. You will most likely find this to be very motivating for your admin and adding a new quality to your collaboration.

On Vacation

To not have to worry about things at work every day when you're on vacation, have your admin cover your email inbox while you are away.

Your admin will scan incoming email and take one of the following actions:

1. If an email can be handled by them or another team member, then the message is forwarded to that team member and then moved to your CC folder (see page 188), so that you can take note of it when you come back.

2. If the email can wait until you come back, then your admin will leave it in your inbox. Priority items may receive a flag, so that you consider them first thing once you come back.

3. If an incoming message is urgent and requires your immediate attention, your admin can alert you in a pre-agreed way (e.g. with a text message or a short phone call).

The procedures above should allow you to not have to check your email every day while you are on vacation. With that, the new system can help you not only in the office, but also while you're out.

Time Saved:

Fifteen minutes a day, meaning **fifty hours saved a year.**

Links:

How to share a folder with your admin:

bit.ly/mb-5011a

How to grant your admin access to your inbox:

bit.ly/mb-5011b

Key Takeaways:

1. Create a shared folder for your admin and use it for emails you wish to delegate to them without further comment.

2. Give your admin access to your email inbox and let them handle email while you are at the office, as well as while you're on vacation.

3. Trust your new system and don't check your email every day while you are on vacation.

12. Dealing with Email: Being a Good Email Citizen

Few things in today's life have the power to cause as much grief as email. Admittedly, it is fast, it is convenient, it is ubiquitous—it is easy to abuse, it is easy to misuse and it can easily make you look foolish, and put a severe dent in your Life Balance.

Here are the top five no-nos that can make you the butt of water-cooler snark; the top five things you can do to be popular, and two useful tips for yourself.

The Top Five No-Nos That Will Come Back to Haunt You

Don't be the one the company giggles about! Avoid these pitfalls:

1. Confidentiality

Be careful when sending confidential information via email. Confidential doesn't have to only mean company secrets, it can be any statement about another person you may not want widely spread. Once an email has gone back and forth several times, the confidential statement might become buried in the thread, but don't assume the email won't ever be forwarded to a broader audience and that your unflattering comment will always stay buried.

2. Professionalism

Using email at work is like writing a letter on corporate stationery. Make it a habit to send only work related content from your corporate email address.

3. No Yelling, Flaming, UPPERCASING

There are many ways to be impolite in email. Typing IN ALL UPPERCASE LETTERS could be construed as bad formatting, carelessness or even written shouting. Being rude or harsh to somebody is always worse in email then delivered personally, because the recipient lacks accompanying body language and can easily assume the worst. A rude email addressed to somebody in an email with a wider addressee list becomes the equivalent of corporate-wide humiliation. To make things worse, an angry email can never be pulled back. It's out there and people will save it in special folders and look at it over and over again. So don't write emails when you're irritated or angry.

4. Think Twice Before You Hit 'Reply All'

Reply all might just be the agent of some evil empire. For one, it's often very difficult to see how many people received the email you're currently reading. A simple address entry might represent a distribution list with hundreds or even thousands of recipients in your company. Admittedly, the sender should not put this information into the TO, but rather into the BCC line of their email. Since nobody wants to be the fool who replied all with a message that went on to annoy untold numbers of colleagues, think three times before hitting 'reply all.'

There have been corporate email storms caused by one person replying to all and then a large number of the recipients again replying to all, demanding an end to this all replying. At least, people's sense of humor stayed intact.

5. Building Important Messages in Offline Mode

There are emails, there are important emails, and then there are very important emails. If you have to write one of the latter, such as an announcement to a large audience or a launch email for an important initiative, switch your email program into offline mode while you prepare it. Few things are more embarrassing than a half-ready milestone email being sent prematurely because you accidentally hit the wrong button.

The Top Five Slick Habits That Will Make You Popular

Here are a few things you can do to amass some email brownie points:

1. No Regular Email on Weekends or at Odd Hours

Ideally, you should not have to do any email during your weekends or outside of office hours. However, some companies have a culture of late night and weekend emails that may be difficult for you to change by yourself. The least you can do is to not send regular emails downwards into your organization. You might find it necessary to reply to an email you receive from your superiors, but don't carry this bad habit on into your team by sending non-urgent information that could wait until the next morning or Monday. If you feel that you have to work on the weekends to catch up on your email, then do so in offline mode and wait to send out your emails on Monday. Otherwise, the signal you send to your team is that they are expected to work on weekends as well.

2. Have Tree Address Lines

You should be very clear on who you want to put on your 'To,' 'CC,' and 'BCC' line.

- The 'To' line is for everyone who needs to react to your email.

- This 'CC' line is for everyone who needs to know the content of your email, but doesn't need to react.

  o In large email threads it is the responsibility of each sender to review the 'To' and 'CC' lines and make changes to them as the conversation evolves. Don't automatically include everyone on the original distribution list even after the conversation has taken a significant turn.

- The 'BCC' line has three purposes:
    - First, large distribution lists should be put here to avoid a mail storm if one recipient accidentally clicks on reply all. It is common to start your message in that case by listing the addressees in the (invisible) 'BCC' line, so that every recipient understands the audience of the particular email.
    - Secondly, the 'BCC' line allows you to enter your own name if you want to find this message in your inbox for further action.
    - Lastly, the 'BCC' line is so that a disguised third-party can be privy to the conversation in your email. 'Disguised' does rightfully imply a certain sneakiness, so use the 'BCC' line very carefully–or not at all–in this way.

3. Break the Thread with a Phone Call

Speaking about long email threads, they should not exist! Email is the communication tool for straightforward information. If you start having a game of email ping-pong, save yourself and the other party some time, pick up the phone and have a conversation on the topic.

4. No Bad or Disturbing News Over Email

If you have bad or disturbing news, email is not the right channel. If the bad news is addressed to one person or a few people, call or meet them in person. If you need to make an announcement to a larger group, choose a meeting either in person or virtually with ample time to see the verbal and non-verbal effects to the communicated information as well as ask questions. You can then follow up with a written version of the information via email.

5. Take a Personal Tone

Email is so fast and so efficient; it tends to be more sparse and free of personal touches than formal letters. That's good but it can also be bad. While you want your email to be as concise as possible, there's something to be said for a friendly greeting, a positive closing, and a clarifying emoticon if there's a risk of the recipient missing the appropriate tone. One emoticon—but not more than one in a single email! :)

If you're sending email from your handheld device, you will most likely not do any of the above. In that case, make sure you have a footer line defined for emails coming from your mobile device to explain the brevity of your message. One example is "sent from my handheld please excuse brevity or typos."

A Tip to Keep You Happy

Periods Without Email

Three kinds of email free periods you should treat yourself to:

Per Day

Define periods during your day you want to dedicate to email—don't have email dictate your day. Deactivate new email notifications on your computer to not be distracted by every incoming message. Determine what times you wish to set aside for reading and answering email, such as an hour in the morning and an hour in the afternoon and don't pay attention to emails outside of those periods.

Per Week

Have email free times in your week. Of course, evenings and weekends should be email free already, but you can also consider a *Project Wednesday Afternoon* without email or a *Strategy Friday Morning* when your Outlook stays closed. You will quickly find these stretches becoming periods of heightened productivity once you get away from the distraction of email.

Per Month

Do the same for your month! If you want to start a new project, or have some quiet time to brainstorm, try to block out a whole day from email and watch your focus and creativity increase.

Key Takeaways:

1. Avoid the pitfalls above when handling your work email.
2. Become more courteous on email by following the tips that will make you more popular with your colleagues.
3. Reward yourself with some real quality working time by setting up email-free zones in your day, your week and your month.

13. Easily Create Meaningful Agendas

 How It Improves Your Life Balance

 The *Agenda Builder* is a free tool I created to take the stress out of creating a useful meeting agenda.

The tool makes it easy to draft, refine, complete and change an agenda without the usual hassle.

1. Download the latest version here: bit.ly/mb-5013
2. Use column A and B to sort agenda items into units of days and units within a day.
3. Use column E to determine an item's length.
4. Add and remove lines as you wish (but make sure to copy or update formulas into the calculating fields as you do).

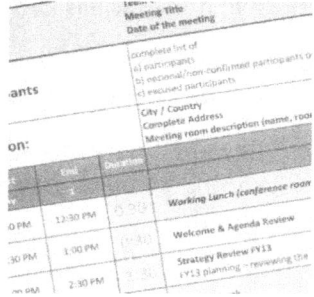

5. Before printing, sort your agenda by selecting the rows with agenda items and choosing the sort function from your data tab in Excel. Sort by A first then B to group days and sort items.
6. If you wish, you can hide column A and B before sending the document. If you print your agenda, these columns will not print.

More Cool Things

Now you can easily...

- ... add new items to your agenda. Simply insert a line, copy the formulas from the line above, enter the information and re-sort your agenda.

- ... delete items. Simply delete the line and update the reference in the line below.
- ... change the duration of an item. Simply enter the new duration in column E and immediately see the impact on the following agenda items.
- ... change the order of agenda items.
- ... change only column A and B and re-sort your agenda.

Link

Download the latest version here: bit.ly/mb-5013

Three ways to use it:

1. Create profound agendas with complete information and objectives for a better meeting.
2. Make hassle-free changes to your agenda. This is particularly useful for larger events with an evolving agenda.
3. Easily reuse and adapt previous meetings' agenda for an upcoming event.

14. Managing Meetings Across Time Zones

Virtual meetings across several time zones are often a big challenge for the organizer and participants alike. Finding a suitable time for that call with team members in San Francisco, London, and Sydney is an almost impossible task at times and some participants almost always end up spending odd morning or late night hours in the meeting.

On the other hand we all want to work in a company that values our contribution independent of where we are based. Our regional insights should be heard in global decisions and we should be able to advance our careers independently of our ability to relocate.

If you are either an organizer or a participant in this game of juggling meeting time zones, here are a few things to consider:

- When running a global team with recurring meetings across time zones, be fair and rotate the burden of after-hour participation.

- Find out your participants' taboo times (e.g. family times or core sleeping hours) and try to accommodate everyone when possible.

- Find two or three different times that gives participants a mix of good and bad meeting times and then rotate to be fair.

- Be extra diligent in having an efficient agenda and important topics to discuss. Consider canceling a meeting if nothing important is on the list. Some of your participants are paying a higher price to join the meeting and you want it to be worthwhile.

- As a participant make sure you join the meeting or send a proxy. You might be wasting everyone's time if decisions have to be postponed because you are missing the call. If you know that you will be missing a meeting, let the organizer know as soon as possible so that he or she can consider canceling the meeting.

When running one-time meetings, much of the above applies as well. In addition:

- As an organizer, be very specific about who needs to be on the call (those who go into the TO line of the invitation) and who is an optional participant (those who go into the CC line).

- As a participant, be courteous in responding to meeting invitations immediately or as soon as possible. This way the organizer can react swiftly and reschedule if too many participants are unavailable.

Other things to consider:

As an Organizer

Here is a useful resource to plan events across time zones: bit.ly/mb-5014a

As a Participant

Be aware that organizers will try to invite you to as many meeting as they deem necessary and at the times that suit them. While this is fair game, be the owner of your calendar and clearly communicate if you think that you should not be on that call or if the time does not work for you. While being helpful and cooperative, you still must define for yourself how many late night and early morning calls you can take while maintaining a balanced life. Only go beyond your boundaries in rare exceptions; otherwise defend what you have defined for yourself. The organizers of meetings cannot know your boundaries, so you have to take care of alerting them.

Key Takeaways:

1. In recurring team meetings across time zones, be fair and rotate the plan.

2. As an organizer, pay extra attention to ensure an efficient agenda and the right people invited.

3. As a participant, communicate your boundaries and defend them in most cases.

15. Only Have Efficient Meetings

Meetings are work and they often take up a large chunk of time for many of us. Ask yourself how efficient any meeting you participate in is—just think about how much extra time you'd get back to do other important things if you were able to reduce meeting times and influence them to be more productive.

Your meeting destiny is at least partially in your own hands—here are a few things to consider making your meetings more efficient:

- Make sure the meetings you set up have a clear agenda with an objective in the invite. If the ones you get invited to don't have one, ask for it so that you can decide whether or not to attend.

- Take minutes and document the meeting outcome and send them to the meeting attendees with actions required, deadlines, and other relevant information clearly stated.

- Wrap up your meeting five minutes early.

- Keep meetings to the minimum time—45 minutes is better than 60.

- Have you tried standing meetings? Decisions get made faster when nobody gets to sit!

- Designate one day per week as meeting-free—Fridays often work for many people as a way to have uninterrupted time to wrap up their week. However, try to choose at least one day that works best for you and schedule it as meeting free. Be disciplined about it and incorporate it into your weekly schedule to make it productive and meaningful time.

- Practice conference room meeting discipline: arrive for in-person meetings five minutes before they begin and wrap up five minutes before the end time to ensure you complete your agenda before you must leave the conference room.
- Hold shorter meetings—with a clear agenda, you can accomplish much in fifteen minutes.
- Minimize the list of participants to only those crucial to the objective.
- Prepare your content in writing (ppt, notes, a napkin, mind map, etc.) prior to the meeting—do not use the meeting to clarify your ideas, unless the purpose of the meeting is specifically to brainstorm.
- Hold others accountable for all of the above.

Check out these resources for more ideas on how to improve your meeting experiences:

- Forbes Magazine: 4 Steps to Fast, Effective Meetings: bit.ly/mb-5015

Key Takeaways:

1. Identify how your meetings can be more efficient to save you and others time.
2. Hold others accountable when they invite you to meetings.

16. Have a Three Minute Version

 Are you ready for that important meeting where you will present your idea? Are your slides polished, the presentation well-rehearsed? Did you even bring a spare projector, just in case? You're ready for anything, but are you prepared for your 45 minute time slot to melt down to three minutes?

The larger the company the larger the decision-making bodies and the more elaborate the meetings where important decisions are being made. If you have successfully made it onto the agenda for one of these milestone meetings and you are ready to present your great idea, make sure to have a fully functional package that you can present within three to five minutes.

Big meetings are likely to be considerably behind schedule. By the time you set up, there's a big chance you will be presented with the option to either come back for the next meeting—or use the remaining time slot. This could be ten minutes before lunch is served.

For these situations, always be prepared to use the time offered, no matter how short it is. The next meeting might be weeks away and you would be losing valuable time. Being able to concisely present your idea, your suggested course of action, and even leave a few minutes for questions, will most likely impress everyone in the room.

If, at the end of your five minute session, you have achieved your objective and gotten the go-ahead, you won't even care about the wonderful slides that got left to the way-side.

Key Takeaways:

1. When planning for an important presentation, be prepared for a time slot much shorter than what you originally anticipated.

2. Be flexible—and ready to present in any time slot offered you.

3. Do not exceed the allocated time, unless the head of the meeting says it's okay.

17. Make Your Breaks Social

Take a moment to think about your lunch break at work. Does it consist of take-out or a sandwich at your desk during a conference call or while answering emails? Change your habit and take a real lunch break for some immediate benefits.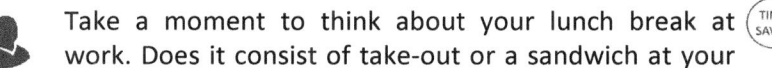

Re-energize for a Productive Afternoon

Taking a short break for lunch every day will help you recharge your batteries and clean your mind for a productive afternoon. It's a misconception that you can save time by eating at your desk. How productive can you be, eating and working and worrying about potentially staining either your documents or your equipment? Instead, meet with colleagues, have some social time and actually enjoy your food. You will return to your desk more productive for the rest of the day.

Pay Attention to What You Eat

If it's true that you are what you eat, then paying more attention to a healthy and well-balanced diet at work can be a big plus. The things you can carry back to your desk are not always the healthiest options. Also, combining eating with another task has been proven to result in overeating and a lack of satisfaction when the meal is over. Instead, focus on your meal and then on your mail separately. You'll be more aware of your messages and more able to listen to your body so as not to overeat.

Be Social and Network Over Lunch

Your lunch break is a great opportunity to mingle and socialize with your colleagues and team members; a chance to let them get to know you as a person. Non-work related conversations over lunch help to see the individual in the people you work with. It also makes you more authentic and helps others come to trust you.

Don't underestimate the amount of work related and informal office related information being exchanged over lunch breaks. Don't miss that social interaction; rather, benefit from maintaining your network in a fun way.

Need Some Alone Time?

If you don't feel like company and need some alone time on a crazy day, instead of hiding at your desk, get up and go for a walk—ideally in a natural environment. If you're tired, consider taking a short nap. Many office buildings nowadays have rooms that provide a place for this. Listen to what your body needs to get ready for the second half of your workday.

Key Takeaways:

1. Make sure to take a proper lunch break; don't work and eat at the same time.
2. Choose your food consciously and listen to what your body needs.
3. Be social and mingle or—if you feel like it —treat yourself to a brief walk or a nap to recharge for the second half of the day.

18. Share Your Screen During a Phone Call

  When you're on the phone with someone discussing work on your computer, why not let the other person see what you're talking about? A program called join.me lets you read out or send a short link that allows the person on the other line to see your screen just like you do.

How It Improves Your Life Balance

With join.me you can have anyone with a computer look at your screen at the same time as you do. It's great for explaining something on screen and helpful to share work in progress without sending it out. It even helps you collaborate by taking notes during a virtual meeting with everyone following along.

More Cool Things

- As the person who starts the sharing, there is no sign-up process and a very small download. You start your sharing session by clicking on the downloaded file.

- The other person who looks at your screen need only type a very short URL into their browser, and off they go.

- It's completely free of charge and doesn't come with advertising banners.

Link

www.join.me

Three ways to use it:

1. Use it to show, not just explain, to someone what you are doing on your computer.
2. Share work in progress without having to send it out.
3. Collaborate by taking notes in a virtual meeting with everyone following along.

19. Working in a Global Team

In today's work environment, the chances that you will someday work in a global team are high. While being on an international team is exciting, exposes you to views and cultures from around the globe, and opens new career opportunities, it can also present some challenges. Since meeting in person can be difficult and expensive, you'll most likely be organizing virtual meetings to keep team members aligned. Because working together remotely and collaborating virtually can be difficult, you will need some dedicated tools.

Working Together Virtually

Working together virtually means a lot of time spent on conference calls. On these calls you will share your voice, potentially a video of yourself or other participants, as well as materials such as slides or demos, through some type of software.

Voice: Hearing Each Other

Whether working virtually with one other person or an entire team, you'll want to make sure that your counterparts can hear you well. If you spend a lot of time on conference calls, it makes sense to invest in a high-quality headset. Few things are worse than spending an hour on a conference call with your handset locked between your head and your shoulder or your speakerphone howling and disturbing everyone in your office or home. My personal preferred headset, the Plantronics Savi Office (see link at the end of this chapter), connects to my PC and my telephone. It's good for phone calls, Skype, video streaming and webinars.

If you participate in virtual meetings on your mobile phone, make sure to get a quality headset for that as well (again, see the link at the bottom of this chapter) and keep the background noise in mind, e.g. while walking through an airport terminal or driving your car. When your environment is noisy, mute yourself when you're not speaking. Also, make sure to familiarize yourself with the telephone's functions on your landline and your mobile phone. This includes the mute function, as well as how to increase and decrease volume both for the speaker and the listener.

For conference calls with many participants, you will have to use a conference call dial-in number. I personally also like using a conference call dial-in number for one-on-one phone meetings. The advantage is that the participants usually have dial-in numbers for several countries, allowing them to efficiently participate even when traveling. In addition, I like not ending up on someone's answering machine if they're not yet ready for the conversation. With a conference call number, everyone dials in at their own pace and you can do something else while you wait for your colleagues to arrive.

If you work in a large firm, your employer probably provides conference call dial-in numbers to you. Should you not have them, there are several conference call providers offering very reasonable quality. Google to find them online, free of charge or see one example link at the end of this chapter.

Multi-Tasking on Conference Calls?

Don't multi-task on a one-on-one call! If the conversation isn't worth your undivided attention anymore, then wrap it up and end it. However, when a larger group gets together, there will quite naturally be phases of the meeting that are not relevant to you. This time can be efficiently used to attend to your email, clean up your desk, sort files etc. The challenge is to keep an ear in the conversation so that you can turn your undivided attention back into the call once it is relevant to you again.

Video: Using a Webcam

Webcams add a nice personal touch to virtual collaboration. I've managed virtual teams for more than fifteen years and always enjoyed webcams in one-on-one conversations with people I haven't seen in a long time or as a tool to introduce myself to someone I have not met before.

On the other hand, they may not be so helpful in calls with many participants, for participants joining from their mobile device, or in routine meetings consisting of a brief conversation. The video feed consumes a lot of bandwidth, which sometimes will impact your audio connection negatively. Also, using a webcam can be quite invasive for participants joining from different time zones or from home office environments. Pajamas or bed-head can make the experience embarrassing for someone who needs to call at an odd hour.

Make sure you agree on certain basic webcam etiquette within your team, and always ask before you use a webcam. When you do use one, make sure you have a professional, tidy background that does not distract from the conversation.

Material: Sharing Material Virtually During a Meeting

There are several ways to share material like PowerPoint presentations documents or software demos during the virtual meeting. More structured services like WebEx or Microsoft Live Meeting allow you to upload your content prior and then share it very professionally during your virtual meeting.

Other tools like join.me (see page 217) allow you to spontaneously share your screen with other participants and collaboratively fill in an Excel sheet, show a software demo or teach somebody a new trick on your PC. I personally love join.me, as it is a very small download for you and does not involve any download or account creation for participants who want to look at your shared desktop.

Time Zones

Managing your virtual meetings across several time zones is a whole topic in and of itself. I have created a separate chapter for this, which can be found on page 208.

Creating a Shared Workspace

If you collaborate virtually with other team members, you will benefit from a place where you can store documents and files that you need for your work. Emailing everything back and forth not only clogs up your email system, it can get difficult to organize and can add a lot of confusion regarding different versions of the same document.

If you work in a larger company, you will probably have shared workspace available in the form of an FTP server or a SharePoint site. Go through the effort of finding out how these systems work to get the most benefit from them.

Small organizations can easily set up shared workspaces with free tools such as Dropbox (www.dropbox.com) or Norton Zone (www.nortonzone.com). Both systems are similar and easy to use. They also allow you to access the shared files from all kinds of devices including your handheld and your desktop. I personally prefer the user-friendly Dropbox, but if you're working with more sensitive information, the more secure Norton Zone might be for you.

Meeting Face to Face with Your Virtual Team

If your team gets a chance to come together in person then there are a few things to keep in mind:

- Carefully plan ahead for your face-to-face meetings. Secure the budget for them and combine the necessary travel with other meetings, visits and projects to make the T&E expense more worthwhile.

- Use technology to your advantage. Skype and webcams can make up for some good face-to-face time when meeting one-on-one or in small teams.

- When dialing-in colleagues for meetings that have several participants in the room, consider broadcasting a video-feed from the meeting room, e.g. via Skype. It adds a lot for the person(s) on the phone and helps them understand what's going on in the room and stay engaged.

- If your site has a dedicated video conferencing room (e.g. HALO), understand how to book and use it and make a point of trying it for a major meeting or discussion.

- Check-out the *Agenda Builder* on page 206 to take the hassle out of building a meaningful agenda for your meeting.

Links:

Link to the headset for use with your PC as well as your phone: bit.ly/mb-5019a

Link to a Bluetooth headset for your mobile phone: bit.ly/mb-5019b

Link to a sample provider of free conference calling services: www.freeconferencecall.com

Key Takeaways:

1. Get the right tools for your virtual meetings.
2. Create a shared workspace for material you need in your team.
3. Plan your rare real-life meeting with care—they are precious for a virtual team.

Part 6 Resources

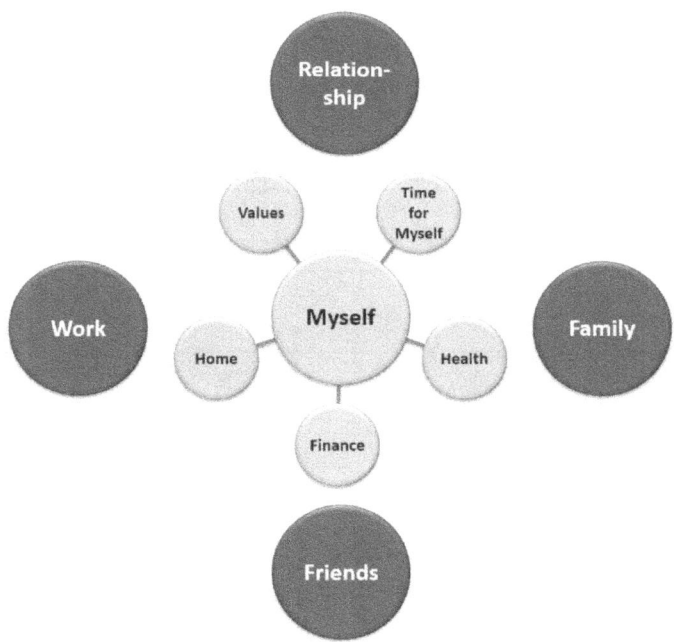

1. Your Life Balance Improvement Plan

You can use this list for building your Personal Life Balance Improvement Plan. Just check whether (👍) or not (👎) a particular tip resonated for you and–if it did–check it off (✓) once you feel that you have mastered this advice.

See the next chapter for a coupon code in case you would like to create this plan online on mybalance.net.

		👎	👍	✓
	Life Balance Advice for Yourself			
TIME SAVER	1. Find the Time			
	2. Do You Get Enough Tranquility?			
TIME SAVER	3. Important Things First			
TIME SAVER	4. Block Time for Important Things			
TIME SAVER	5. Shut Up Your Gadgets			
	6. Introduction to Meditation			
TIME SAVER	7. Working from Home is Not Easy			
	8. 1,000 Places to See Before You Die			
	9. Workout Music in Style			
TIME SAVER	10. Stop Wasting Time at Your PC			

	👎	👍	✓
11. Remote Troubleshoots			
12. Values, Ethics, Faith, Religion			
13. Too Much Suffering in the World?			
14. Are You Two Kinds of Happy?			
15. Look Up for Motivation			
16. Treat People with Kindness			
17. Depolarize			
18. The Book of Awakening			
19. The Diamond Cutter			
20. A Very Pragmatic Approach			
21. Preview Your Deathbed			
22. Beyond Religion			
23. Guide to the Bodhisattva's Way of Life			
24. De-Clutter Your Lifestyle			
25. When in Debt, Change Your Life			

TIME SAVER

	👎	👍	✓
26. Review Your Recurring Spending			
27. Self-Employed and Successful			
28. Are You Relatively Poor?			
29. Don't Fly Blind Financially			
30. Do You Have the Right Home?			
31. My Home is My (Affordable) Castle			
32. De-Clutter Your Life			
(TIME SAVER) 33. Is Your Home a Chore or Hobby?			
(TIME SAVER) 34. Commuting to Work			
(TIME SAVER) 35. Get a Robot to Help in Your Garden			
(TIME SAVER) 36. A Space Age Vacuum Cleaner			
37. When Being Healthy Is Not Achievable			
38. Sleep Well			
39. Thoughts Before You Sleep			
40. Eat Well and Exercise			

	👎	👍	✓
41. Explore Alternative Medicine			
42. Stop Sitting			
43. Don't Worry About Stress			
44. Your Recharge Toolbox			
45. Burn Away Your Mosquito Bites			
46. Is Your Scale Online?			
Life Balance Advice for Your Relationships			
1. Alone Time with Your Partner			
2. Trip of Love—Looking for Places to Go?			
3. Time Without Your Devices			
4. Plan Your Vacation Carefully			
5. On People Who Want to Be Unhappy			
6. Caring For Your Elderly Parents			
7. Hands-Free Timesavers			
8. The Five Essential Truths About Friendship			

		👎	👍	✓
	9. How to Make New Friends			
	10. The Five Essential Things to Maintain Friendships			
	11. Tools for Staying in Touch			
Life Balance Advice for Your Work				
TIME SAVER	1. Reduce Your Worklist			
TIME SAVER	2. Decide When and Where You Work!			
TIME SAVER	3. 15 Things To Work Smarter			
TIME SAVER	4. Delegate			
	5. Make Sure You Like Your Work			
TIME SAVER	6. Dealing with Email: Manage the Flood			
TIME SAVER	7. Dealing with Email: Tune Your Spam Engine			
TIME SAVER	8. Dealing with Email: CCs Go Separate			
TIME SAVER	9. Dealing with Email: Stop Using (Most) Folders			
TIME SAVER	10. Dealing with Email: Know Your Device			
TIME SAVER	11. Dealing with Email: Working with Your Admin			

	👎	👍	✓
12. Dealing with Email: Being a Good Email Citizen			
13. Easily Create Meaningful Agendas				*TIME SAVER*
14. Managing Meetings Across Time Zones				*TIME SAVER*
15. Only Have Efficient Meetings				*TIME SAVER*
16. Have a Three Minute Version				*TIME SAVER*
17. Make your Breaks Social				*TIME SAVER*
18. Share Your Screen During a Phone Call				*TIME SAVER*
19. Working in a Global Team			

2. Your Coupon for mybalance.net

Get This Book Free of Charge

If you like the content of this book and intend to improve your Life Balance, then mybalance.net is for you!

mybalance.net is the web's leading destination to assess and enhance your Life Balance.

Only Here Will You Find:

- A profound assessment of your personal Life Balance Score™.
- All the down-to-earth tips from this book – and more – in an easy to navigate Advice Center with plenty of filter and sorting features.
- A community to share and vet ideas with.
- A diary app to track your own progress.

All this makes mybalance.net fun, useful and helps you to live a more mindful life.

Get this book for free!

If you would like to join mybalance.net to take your Life Balance Check™ or build your personal Life Balance Improvement Plan, then we won't charge you twice: use the coupon code

BOOK-6856

while purchasing your mybalance membership and we will deduct the price of this book from your membership fee.

3. Recharge Toolbox Tear-Out Sheet

Wall Version

Fifteen Great Ways to Re-Energize during the Day

1. Be outside
2. Exercise
3. Take a nap
4. Read something pleasant or inspiring
5. Slow down and do one thing at a time
6. Be silent and give your thoughts some room
7. Have a good conversation
8. Change your point of view
9. Show compassion
10. Imagine something new
11. Ask someone for help
12. Fix a small nuisance
13. Let go of something
14. Meet a new person
15. Perform an act of kindness
16. Enjoy (!) a meal

Wallet Version

**Fifteen Great Ways to
Re-Energize during the Day**

1. Be outside
2. Exercise
3. Take a nap
4. Read something pleasant or inspiring
5. Slow down and do one thing at a time
6. Be silent and give your thoughts some room
7. Have a good conversation
8. Change your point of view
9. Show compassion
10. Imagine something new
11. Ask someone for help
12. Fix a small nuisance
13. Let go of something
14. Meet a new person
15. Perform an act of kindness
16. Enjoy (!) a meal

www.mybalance.net

4. About the Author

Stefan Osthaus has been a leader in Fortune 500 companies for more than 15 years. He has held global responsibility for the customer experience of tens of millions of customers as well as the employee experience of thousands of employees. Stefan is a global keynote speaker and the founder of mybalance.net.

Having observed people complain about the lack of "work-life-balance" throughout his decades of leadership experience, Stefan turned his passion to help improve balance for others into dedication to provide Life Balance advice to users, audiences and corporate employees around the world.

Prior to founding mybalance.net, Stefan worked with the Japanese electronics giant Canon and the world's fourth largest software maker Symantec for over twenty years. He has held several leadership positions including VP Worldwide Marketing, VP Customer Care as well as VP Customer & Employee Experience. His work with employees to provide a sustainable balance in all aspects of work and beyond has created a wealth of insight and advice now made available on mybalance.net, via Stefan's publications and in his keynote speeches.

You can contact Stefan and his team via email at team@mybalance.net.

www.ingramcontent.com/pod-product-compliance
Lightning Source LLC
Chambersburg PA
CBHW051801170526
45167CB00005B/1835